# PATRICK LOSE'S

# Special Delivery

## QUILTS

C&T PUBLISHING

*CADCC* SC

Developmental Editor: Barbara Konzak Kuhn
Technical Editor: Joyce Engels Lytle
Cover Design: Kristen Yenche
Book Design: Kristen Yenche
Front cover quilt: "Rub A Dub Dub"
Illustrator: Alan McCorkle © C&T Publishing
Photography: Sharon Risedorph

**Library of Congress Cataloging-in-Publication Data**
Lose, Patrick.
Special delivery quilts / Patrick Lose.
    p. cm.
    Includes index.
    ISBN 1-57120-088-6 (paper trade)
    1. Appliqué--Patterns. 2. Quilting--Patterns. 3. Crib quilts. 4. Wall hangings. I. Title.
TT779 .L6823 2000
746.46'041--dc21

99-050515

Published by C&T Publishing, Inc.
P.O. Box 1456
Lafayette, California 94549

Printed in China
10 9 8 7 6 5 4 3 2 1

# Special Delivery
# QUILTS

# Dedication

To Katie: You'll always be my "baby."

# Acknowledgments

I'd like to thank the following people for their part in creating this book:

Lenny Houts, whose perfect craftsmanship shows in each of these quilts.

Shon Jones, for her talented work on *Pretty in Pastels*.

Marti and Dick Michell, for providing us with Perfect Patchwork System templates and for their invaluable "tips" on using them.

Gayle Boshek and Vivian Irwin, for their friendship and support.

And, most of all, the entire team at C&T Publishing for once again presenting my work in such a beautiful way.

# Introduction

I've spent a lot of time around babies. I love them. Although I've only been father to one, there was always one around as I was growing up. That's because I'm the eldest of eight siblings. I have five brothers and two sisters, all born in a span of less than twelve years. The five oldest were all born within five years. One of my brothers and one of my sisters are eight days short of a year apart. Two of my brothers are twins. Because of this, my parents had four babies in diapers at the same time. This, at least, should make them eligible for Sainthood. But, obviously, they love babies too. It's a good thing, they have seven grandchildren...and another on the way.

So, as I said, I've spent a lot of time around babies. They are the inspiration for this book.

Anticipating the arrival of a baby always brings the desire to create a wonderful nursery. I've heard from so many of my friends and relatives that they wish they could make their own quilts for their "bundles of joy." With so many beginner classes available at quilt shops, and so many patterns and ideas on the market from quilt designers, the time has never been better to take the first step in learning.

Within this book, you'll surely find several quilts that are perfect for a first-time quilting project. In fact, I've tried to make sure that none of the quilt designs offered are too difficult or too time consuming to make. We all know that those nine months of waiting brings lots of other things to do besides sewing! But what better way to pass the time and to welcome your special delivery?

# Table of Contents

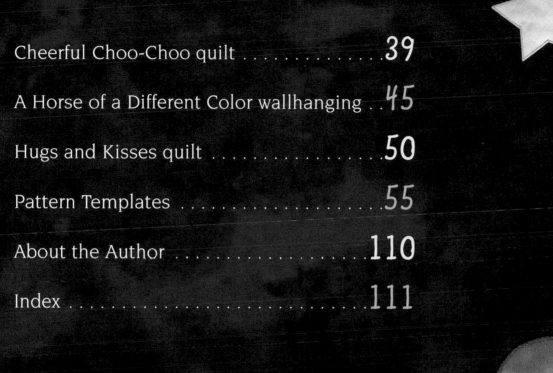

# General Instructions

## General Sewing

All the projects in *Special Delivery Quilts* are sewn using a $1/4$" seam allowance and are stitched with the fabrics placed right sides together. As tempting as it may be to "jump" right into your project, it is always best to read all of the instructions thoroughly before you begin.

## Tools

Make sure you have all the necessary tools at hand before you start cutting and stitching up a storm. It's easy to let your excitement for the project get the best of you, and then you're off to the quilt shop to buy more fabric or to hunt for a seam ripper! Following is a list of helpful tools that will make your stitching easier.

---

- Rotary cutter and cutting mat
- Transparent acrylic gridded ruler
- Scissors for cutting fabric
- Scissors for cutting paper
- Safety Pins
- Hand sewing needles
- Permanent black marker with an ultra fine tip such as a Pigma Micron® or IDentipen® for marking templates and patterns

- Light box, if desired
- Machine sewing needles, size 80
- Chaco-Liner® for marking quilting lines
- Seam ripper
- Sewing machine capable of doing satin stitch or narrow zigzag stitch.
- Walking foot for machine quilting
- Darning foot for free-motion quilting
- Iron

## Fabrics

I don't pre-wash any of my fabrics for quilting. This is my personal preference based on my never having had a problem with any of the colors bleeding. If I do wash the finished piece, the minimal shrinkage creates a slightly puckered quilt with a softer look and feel. There are those who always pre-wash, and that is perfectly fine. Just be sure that, if you pre-wash, you do it in warm water to allow the fabric to shrink as much as it is going to. Tumble dry and remove from the dryer when the fabric is still slightly damp. Always iron the fabric before measuring and cutting. Do not use starch on fabrics that will be used for appliqué pieces. It could make fabric difficult to fuse.

It is extremely important to measure and cut your fabrics accurately and to stitch using an exact $1/4$" seam allowance. I am certain you'll be proud of your finished piece if you follow these simple rules.

## Appliqué

The appliqué projects in this book use a fusible-adhesive appliqué method and are outlined using a machine satin or zigzag stitch. Should you wish to do hand appliqué (knock yourself out…), you'll need to add seam allowances to the appliqué patterns.

All of the patterns in this book for appliqué are printed actual size and are reversed for tracing onto paper-backed fusible adhesive. Be sure to use a lightweight paper-backed fusible adhesive that is suitable for sewing.

For a couple of the projects, I have used a permanent black marker to color the pupils of the eyes. To keep the marker from bleeding, it helps to blow on the area as you are marking.

## Quilting

I like to use a single layer of thin cotton batting such as Warm & Natural®. Cut your backing fabric and batting to measure 2" to 3" larger than your quilt top on all sides. (I allow 2" extra on all sides for small projects and 3" extra on all sides for the larger projects.)

Sandwich the batting between the top and backing, wrong sides together, and baste through all layers, smoothing the quilt top outward from the center. You can also use safety pins spaced about 4"-6" apart.

All of the quilting in this book was done by machine. I use a walking foot for quilting. For free-motion or stipple quilting, use a darning foot and lower the feed dogs on your machine. That doesn't mean you can't quilt by hand if you'd like; hand quilting would be a beautiful addition to the look of these pieces. You may quilt as desired or refer to the photos and quilting suggestions that are included with each project. A Chaco-liner is great for marking quilting lines if you are not comfortable "eyeballing" them, and the lines can be easily brushed away. When quilting appliqué projects, be sure to break the quilting path over all the appliqué shapes.

## Binding

**The instructions for each project give you the amount of binding necessary to finish your quilt project.**

1 I like to use $2\frac{1}{8}$"-wide strips cut selvage to selvage using a rotary cutter, mat, and a transparent acrylic gridded ruler. These strips will measure about 40-44" long, after you have straightened your fabric and cut off the selvages.

2 Use diagonal seams to join binding strips. Trim seam allowance and press the seam open. Fold the completed length of binding in half lengthwise with the wrong sides together. Press.

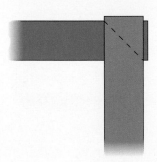

3 Place the folded binding strip on the right side of the quilt top, beginning in the center of one side

and aligning the raw edges of the quilt and the binding. Fold over the beginning of the binding about $1/2$". Stitch through all of the layers using a $1/4$" seam allowance. Stop stitching $1/4$" from the corner. Backstitch two or more stitches, remove the quilt from the machine, and clip the threads.

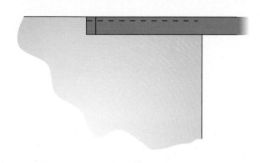

4 Fold the binding up and crease the fold with your fingers.

5 Holding the fold in place, fold the binding down and align the raw edges with the next side of the quilt. Start stitching again at the corner, through all layers. Stitch around the quilt, treating each corner as you did the first.

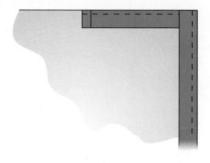

6 When you return to where you started, stitch the binding beyond the fold you made in the strip at the beginning. Backstitch two or more stitches and clip the threads. At this time, cut off the excess batting and backing fabric so that all layers are even.

7 Turn the binding over the quilt edge, aligning the fold of the binding with the machine stitching you just finished. You can pin the binding in place, but I like to use those funny little hair clips that bend/snap closed; they work great

and don't get stuck in the carpet. You can find them at most variety or drugstores under the brand name Goody®. Sew the binding in place by hand onto the backing. Make sure you cover the machine stitching. Miter the corners of the backside of the binding also, stitching the fold in place, if necessary.

Be sure to display your work of art in a conspicuous place where it is most likely to prompt compliments, but keep in mind that direct sunlight will fade fabric more quickly than you might think.

# Our Baby Album

Patrick Lose

Katie Lose

Lenny Houts

Kris Yenche

Sharon Risedorph

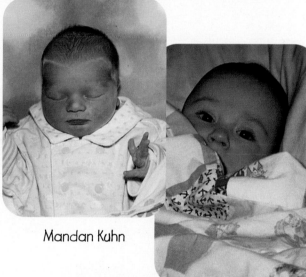

Mandan Kuhn

North Kuhn

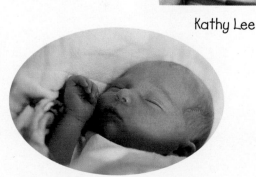

Kathy Lee

Alan McCorkle

Joyce Lytle

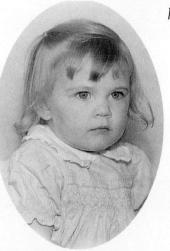

Thomas Hensley

Rub A Dub Dub, 1999.
30 1/2" x 30 1/2"
Designed by Patrick Lose.
Quilt top made and quilted by Lenny Houts.

# Rub A Dub Dub

## Required Fabric and Supplies

- $3/4$ yard lilac: $1/2$ yard for border and bath tub appliqué and $1/4$ yard for binding
- $1 1/8$ yards coral: $1/8$ yard for bath tub appliqué and 1 yard for backing
- $1/3$ yard seafoam (green) for border and bath tub appliqué
- $3/4$ yard aqua for corner squares and center background
- $1/4$ yard medium flesh for baby appliqué
- $2/3$ yard white for suds and bubbles appliqué, and white of duck eye
- 6" square of lemon (yellow) for duck body appliqué
- scrap of orange for duck bill appliqué
- scrap of sky (blue) for duck eye appliqué
- Backing: coral fabric listed above
- Binding: lilac fabric listed above
- Thin cotton batting: 34" x 34"
- 1 yard lightweight paper-backed fusible adhesive
- Thread for piecing
- Tear-away stabilizer
- Matching thread for machine appliqué and quilting
- Black permanent ink pen for eyes

## Cutting Fabrics

Using a rotary cutter, mat, and ruler, cut the following strips selvage to selvage:

### LILAC

Five $1 3/4$"-wide strips for the border.

Four $2 1/8$"-wide strips for binding. Piece the strips together end to end.

### CORAL

Cut backing to measure 34" x 34".

### SEAFOAM (GREEN)

Five $1 3/4$"-wide strips for the border.

### AQUA

One $5 1/2$"-wide strip. From the strip cut four $5 1/2$" squares for the border.

One $20 1/2$" x $20 1/2$" square for the background.

## Fusible Appliqué Preparation

All appliqué pattern pieces for this project are on pages 56-64. They are printed actual size and reversed for tracing onto fusible adhesive. Join the pieces when tracing as indicated on the pattern.

1 Lay the fusible adhesive, paper side up, over each pattern and use

a pencil to trace onto the paper side. Write the pattern number on each piece as you trace.

2 Be sure to trace any appliqué placement lines or detail stitching lines using a permanent marker.

3 Use paper-cutting scissors to roughly cut all the pieces approximately $^1/_4$" outside the traced lines.

4 Following manufacturer's instructions for fusing, fuse the traced pattern onto the wrong side of the fabric (indicated by color).

**Lilac:** wash tub (R2 and R6)

**Coral:** Wash tub (R4)

**Seafoam (Green):** wash tub (R3 and R5)

**Medium Flesh:** baby (R1)

**White:** Suds and bubbles (R7–R11); duck's eye (R14)

**Lemon (Yellow):** duck (R12)

**Orange:** duck's bill (R13)

**Sky (Blue):** duck's eye (R15)

5 Cut out the pieces along the traced lines.

6 Transfer any placement and detail stitching lines to the right side of the fabric using a lightbox and a pencil.

## ASSEMBLING THE QUILT TOP

Note: *With this quilt, you will first need to assemble the entire quilt top, before positioning and fusing the appliqué.*

1 Stitch together 5 strip sets of $1^3/_4$"-wide lilac and seafoam (green) strips as shown. Press seams toward the lilac strip. Cut the strip sets into thirty-two $5^1/_2$" units.

$5^1/_2$"

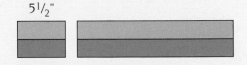

Make 5 strip sets. Cut 32 units.

2 Sew 8 units together for each of the four borders. Press seams toward the lilac fabric.

3 Sew a corner square to each end of two of the border strips for the top and bottom border.

4 Sew the side borders to the center section. Then sew the top and bottom borders to the quilt top.

Quilt Assembly

## POSITION AND FUSE THE APPLIQUÉ PIECES

1 Referring to the photo or illustration for placement, remove the paper backing and position all appliqué pieces onto the quilt top, overlapping some as necessary.

2 When you are satisfied with the placement, fuse the pieces into place, making sure that you smooth the larger pieces as you proceed.

## Satin Stitch Appliqué

Use a tear-away stabilizer on the wrong side of the background fabric. With matching thread suitable for machine appliqué, satin stitch around the appliqué pieces and any detail stitching lines. To satin stitch, use a fairly narrow zigzag stitch and keep your stitch length as close as possible. Stitch over the raw edges of the fused appliqué pieces so that none of the raw edges show. Work outward from the center and smooth the fabric as your proceed.

## Quilting

1 Sandwich the batting between the top and backing, wrong sides together, smoothing the quilt top from the center. Pin baste with safety pins through all layers.

2 Using monofilament thread and a walking foot, stitch around the outside of all satin stitching details and shapes.

3 Using a walking foot, straight stitch the diamond pattern on the tub with matching thread.

4 Using a darning foot, with the machine's feed dogs lowered, stipple the background using matching thread.

5 With the walking foot, stitch-in-the-ditch around the background.

6 Continuing with the walking foot and matching thread, stitch-in-the-ditch along the stripes around the border.

7 Drop the feed dogs once again and with the darning foot, stipple the corner squares.

Bind the quilt referring to the General Instructions, pages 10-12.

Babies come in all colors.

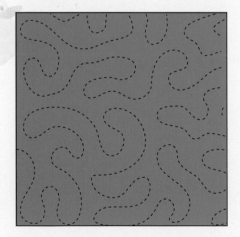

Stippling quilting lines.

Wish Upon A Star, 1999,
38½" x 20½"
Designed by Patrick Lose.
Quilt Top made and quilted by Lenny Houts.

# Wish Upon A Star

## Required Fabric and Supplies

- $1/3$ yard lilac for corner posts and moon nightcap appliqué
- $1/3$ yard powder (blue) for cloud appliqué
- $2/3$ yard chambray (blue) for cloud appliqué and binding
- $3/8$ yard daffodil (yellow) for stars and moon appliqué, and checkered border
- $1/3$ yard peach for stars appliqué and checkered border
- $1^{1}/3$ yards royal (navy) $5/8$ yard for center panel and $2/3$ yard for backing
- Backing: royal (navy) fabric listed above
- Binding: chambray (blue) fabric listed above
- Thin cotton batting: 43" x 25"
- $1^{1}/2$ yards lightweight paper-backed fusible adhesive
- Thread for piecing
- Tear-away stabilizer
- Matching thread for machine appliqué and quilting
- Freezer paper for quilting patterns

## Cutting Fabrics

Using a rotary cutter, mat, and ruler, cut the following strips selvage to selvage:

**LILAC**

One $1^{1}/2$" x 6" strip. From the strip, cut four $1^{1}/2$" squares for corner posts.

**CHAMBRAY (BLUE)**

Four $2^{1}/8$"-wide strips. Piece the strips together end to end for the binding.

**DAFFODIL (YELLOW)**

Three $1^{1}/2$"-wide strips for the border.

**PEACH**

Three $1^{1}/2$"-wide strips for the border.

**ROYAL (NAVY)**

One $36^{1}/2$" x $18^{1}/2$" piece for the center background panel.
One 42" x 24" piece for the backing.

## Fusible Appliqué Preparation

All appliqué pattern pieces for this project are on pages 65-77. They are printed actual size and reversed for tracing onto fusible adhesive. Join the pieces when tracing as indicated on the pattern.

1 Lay the fusible adhesive, paper side up, over each pattern and use a pencil to trace onto the paper side. Write the pattern number on each piece as you trace.

2 Use paper-cutting scissors to roughly cut all the pieces approximately 1" outside the traced lines.

3 Trim the fusible adhesive to within $1/8$" of the inside edge of the traced pattern before fusing it to the fabric.

4 Following manufacturer's instructions for fusing, fuse the traced pattern onto the wrong side of the fabric (indicated by color).

**Lilac:** nightcap (S2)

**Powder (Blue):** clouds (S9 and S10)

**Chambray (Blue):** clouds (S11–S13)

**Daffodil (Yellow):** stars (S4–S6); moon (S1)

**Peach:** stars (S3–S5)

5 Cut out the pieces along the traced lines.

6 Transfer any placement and detail stitching lines to the right side of the fabric using a lightbox and a pencil.

## POSITION AND FUSE THE APPLIQUÉ PIECES

1 Referring to the photo or illustration for placement, remove the paper backing and position all appliqué pieces onto the quilt top, overlapping some as necessary.

2 When you are satisfied with the placement, fuse the pieces into place, making sure that you smooth the larger pieces as you proceed.

## Satin Stitch Appliqué

Use a tear-away stabilizer on the wrong side of the background fabric. With matching thread suitable for machine appliqué, satin stitch around the appliqué pieces and detail lines. To satin stitch, use a fairly narrow zigzag stitch and keep your stitch length as close as possible. Stitch over the raw edges of the fused appliqué pieces so that none of the raw edges show. Work outward from the center and smooth the fabric as you proceed. When the satin stitching is complete, tear away all the stabilizer. If necessary, cut away the excess fabric from the back of the quilt top so that you have one layer remaining on the front. (*Note: Cutting away the fabrics is easy to do but take care not to cut through to the front.*)

## ASSEMBLING THE QUILT TOP

**1** Stitch together 2 strip sets of $1^1/_2$"-wide daffodil (yellow) and peach strips as shown. Press seams toward the peach strip. Cut the strip sets into fifty-four $1^1/_2$" units.

1$^1/_2$"

Make 2 strip sets.

**2** Stitch together eighteen units each for the top and bottom borders. Stitch together nine units each for the side borders. Press seams in one direction.

**3** Sew a lilac corner square to each end of the top and bottom border strips. Press seams toward corner square.

**4** Sew the side borders to the center section. Press seam toward border. Then sew the top and bottom borders to the quilt top. Press seam toward border.

Quilt assembly

# Quilting

1 Sandwich the batting between the top and backing, wrong sides together, smoothing the quilt top from the center. Pin baste with safety pins through all layers.

2 Using monofilament thread and a walking foot, stitch around the outside of all satin stitching details and shapes.

3 Continuing with the walking foot, stitch-in-the-ditch around the inside of the checkerboard border.

4 Position and iron the freezer-paper star patterns onto the navy background. Stitch around the stars with a walking foot and matching thread.

Bind the quilt referring to the General Instructions, pages 10-12.

Twinkle Twinkle Little Star, 1999
36½" x 48½"
Designed by Patrick Lose.
Quilt top made and quilted by Lenny Houts

# Twinkle Twinkle Little Star

## Required Fabric and Supplies

- $2/3$ yard medium blue print for star background
- $2^5/8$ yards medium yellow print: $2/3$ yard for star background, $3/8$ yard for outer border, and $1^1/2$ yards for backing
- 1 yard light blue print: $1/2$ yard for stars, and $1/2$ yard for inner border and binding
- $1/2$ yard light yellow print for stars
- Backing: medium yellow fabric listed above
- Binding: light blue fabric listed above
- Thin cotton batting: 40" x 52"
- Thread for piecing
- Matching thread for machine quilting
- Optional: From Marti Michell Perfect Patchwork Templates, Set B

## Cutting Fabrics

Use templates B-12 and B-14 from template Set B or the following rotary cutting instructions for the star block.

Using a rotary cutter, mat, and ruler, cut the following strips selvage to selvage:

**MEDIUM BLUE PRINT**

Five $2^1/2$"-wide strips. From the strips, cut seventy-two $2^1/2$" squares for star backgrounds.

Three $2^7/8$"-wide strips. From the strips, cut thirty-six $2^7/8$" squares, then cut the squares in half diagonally for star backgrounds.

**MEDIUM YELLOW PRINT**

Five $2^1/2$"-wide strips. From the strips, cut sixty-eight $2^1/2$" squares for star background.

Three $2^7/8$"-wide strips. From the strips, cut thirty-four $2^7/8$" squares, then cut the squares in half diagonally for star background.

Cut five $2^1/2$"-wide strips. Then piece three strips end-to-end and cut two $44^1/2$" lengths for the outer side border.

Cut two 36$\frac{1}{2}$" lengths for the outer top and bottom border from remaining two strips.

Cut backing to measure 40" x 52".

## LIGHT BLUE PRINT

Two 2$\frac{1}{2}$"-wide strips. From the strips, cut seventeen 2$\frac{1}{2}$" squares for star centers.

Three 2$\frac{7}{8}$"-wide strips. From the strips, cut thirty-four 2$\frac{7}{8}$" squares, then cut the squares in half diagonally for star points.

Two 1" x 42" strips for the inner border sides.

Two 1" x 32" strips for the inner border top and bottom.

Five 2$\frac{1}{8}$"-wide strips for the binding. Piece the strips together end-to-end.

## LIGHT YELLOW PRINT

Two 2$\frac{1}{2}$"-wide strips. From the strips, cut eighteen 2$\frac{1}{2}$" squares for star centers.

Three 2$\frac{7}{8}$"-wide strips. From the strips, cut thirty-six 2$\frac{7}{8}$" squares, then cut the squares in half diagonally for star points.

## Assembling Pieced Blocks

### Friendship Star Block

6" finished size

1 Stitch 72 half-square triangle units of the medium blue print and the light yellow. Stitch 68 half-square triangle units of the medium yellow print and light blue print. Press toward light blue triangle.

2 To construct each block, follow the piecing sequence below. Press seams toward the squares. Make 18 yellow-star blocks and 17 blue-star blocks.

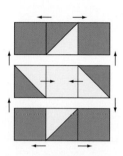

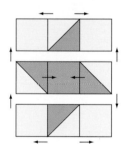

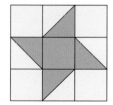

## ASSEMBLING THE QUILT TOP

1 Sew five blocks together to make one row, alternating the block order by color within each row. Make seven rows. Press seams of alternate rows in an opposite direction. This will make sewing the rows together easier.

2 Sew the rows together in a straight setting, as shown. Press seams open.

3 Sew the inner side border strips on the quilt top. Press seams toward the inner border. Then sew the inner top and bottom borders. Press seams toward the inner border. Repeat this order for the outer border.

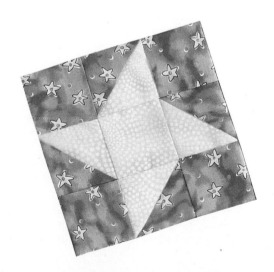

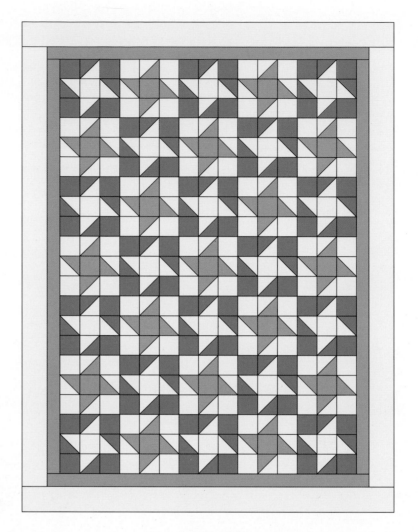

**Quilt assembly**

# Quilting

1 Sandwich the batting between the quilt top and backing, wrong sides together, smoothing the quilt top from the center. Safety pin all seams using a ruler to keep the seams straight.

2 Using a walking foot and monofilament thread, stitch-in-the-ditch around all the blocks and the blue inner border.

3 If desired, you can use matching threads and stitch around each of the stars. We chose not to.

Bind your quilt referring to the General Instructions, pages 10-12.

"I Love You This Much!", 1999,
26½" x 40½"
Designed by Patrick Lose.
Quilt top made and quilted
by Lenny Houts.

# "I Love You This Much!"

## Required Fabric and Supplies

- $1^3/_8$ yards aqua: $1^1/_8$ yards for backing and teddy bear appliqué, $^1/_4$ yards for caption banners
- Scrap piece powder (blue) for bear's ears and nose
- $^1/_8$ yard rose for bear's heart, and 6 hearts in top and bottom borders
- $^5/_8$ yard yellow for background, and 4 stars in top and bottom borders
- $^5/_8$ yards grape: $^3/_8$ yard for sashing, and $^1/_4$ yard for binding
- $^1/_4$ yard aqua print for bear's tummy, muzzle, and paws
- $^1/_8$ yard yellow print with blue polka dot for letters
- Ten $4^1/_2$"squares of three pastel prints for borders
- Backing: aqua fabric listed above
- Binding: grape fabric listed above
- Thin cotton batting: 30" x 44"
- $1^3/_4$ yards lightweight paper-backed fusible adhesive
- Thread for piecing
- Tear-away stabilizer
- Matching thread for appliqué and quilting
- Black permanent ink pen for inking eyes

## Cutting Fabrics

Using a rotary cutter, mat, and ruler, cut the following pieces:

**AQUA**

Two $4^1/_2$" x $24^1/_2$" pieces for caption banners

One 30" x 44" piece for backing. Save the remaining 12" x 44" piece for the teddy bear appliqué pieces.

**YELLOW**

$18^1/_2$" x $24^1/_2$" for background

**GRAPE**

Eight $1^1/_2$"-wide strips, selvage to selvage. Then cut a $40^1/_2$" length from two of the strips for side borders. Cut 24 $^1/_2$" lengths from six of the strips for horizontal sashing. From strip leftovers, cut eight $4^1/_2$" lengths for vertical sashing.

Four $2^1/_8$"-wide binding strips, selvage to selvage. Piece strips together end-to-end.

## Fusible Appliqué Preparation

All appliqué pattern pieces for this project are on pages 78–92. They are printed actual size and reversed for tracing onto fusible adhesive.

1 Lay the fusible adhesive, paper side up, over each pattern and use a pencil to trace onto the paper side. Write the pattern number on each piece as you trace.

2 Be sure to trace any appliqué placement lines or detail stitching lines using a permanent marker.

3 Use paper-cutting scissors to roughly cut all the pieces approximately $1/4$" outside the traced lines.

4 Following manufacturer's instructions for fusing, fuse the traced pattern onto the wrong side of the fabric (indicated by color).

**Aqua:** teddy bear body (L1), head (L2), arms and legs (L3–L6).

**Powder (blue):** bear's ears (L7 and L8) and nose (L9)

**Aqua print:** bear's tummy (L10), muzzle (L11), and paws (L12–L15)

**Yellow print:** 1 each of the letters

**Rose:** bear heart (L16), six border hearts (L17)

**Yellow:** four stars (L18)

5 Cut out the pieces along the traced lines.

6 Transfer any placement and detail stitching lines to the right side of the fabric using a lightbox and a pencil.

### ASSEMBLING THE QUILT TOP

*Note: With this quilt, you will first need to assemble the entire quilt top, before positioning and fusing the appliqué.*

1 Stitch, alternating $4^1/_2$" squares and vertical sashing strips until you have 5 squares joined by 4 sashing strips, as shown. Repeat for the bottom border.

2 Stitch a horizontal sashing strip to the top and bottom of the first border. Repeat for the bottom border, and center section.

3 Join together the banners, center section, and top and bottom borders as shown.

4 Sew the side strips to complete the quilt.

Quilt assembly

## POSITION AND FUSE THE APPLIQUÉ PIECES

1 Referring to the photo or illustration for placement, remove the

paper backing and position all appliqué pieces onto the quilt top, overlapping some as necessary.

2 When you are satisfied with the placement, fuse the pieces into place, making sure that you smooth the larger pieces as you proceed.

3 Instead of using the letters for I Love You This Much!, you may want to personalize your quilt with the baby's name and birthday, or another message. Enlarge the letters and numbers on pages 89-92 to the desired percentage that will work for your message.

## SATIN STITCH APPLIQUÉ

Use tear-away stabilizer on the wrong side of the background fabric. With matching thread suitable for machine appliqué, satin stitch around the appliquéd pieces and detail the stitching lines. To satin stitch, use a fairly narrow zigzag stitch and keep your stitch length as close as possible. Stitch over the raw edges of the fused appliqué pieces so that none of the raw edges show. Work outward from the center and smooth the fabric as you proceed. When the satin stitching is complete, tear away all the stabilizer.

## Quilting

1 Sandwich the batting between the quilt top and backing, wrong sides together, and baste through all layers, smoothing the quilt top outward from the center.

2 Using monofilament thread and a walking foot, stitch around the outside of all satin stitching details and shapes.

3 Using a darning foot, drop the feed dogs on your machine and stipple the background around the bear with matching thread.

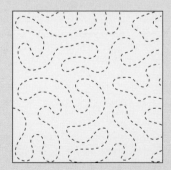

4 With the same thread, switch to a walking foot and stitch-in-the-ditch around the center background.

5 To mark the diagonal grid pattern behind the letters, use a Chaco-liner and a gridded ruler with a 45° line on it. Place the ruler on the sashing at the 45° angle and mark using the Chaco-Liner. Mark the lines 1" apart across the caption banners in both directions. Using the walking foot and matching thread, stitch all lines in both directions stopping at the letters, then jumping over and continue stitching again. Clip all threads.

6 Switch to a walking foot and stitch-in-the-ditch using matching thread around the inside of both caption banner backgrounds.

7 With a ruler and Chaco-Liner, mark an X through the star and heart backgrounds from corner to corner. With matching thread and a walking foot, stitch the lines stopping at the star or heart, jump over and continue to the corner. When the X is stitched, stitch-in-the-ditch around each background. Clip all threads.

8 Bind the quilt referring to the General Instructions, pages 10-12.

Pretty in Pastels quilt, 1999,
43$\frac{1}{4}$" x 43$\frac{1}{4}$"
Designed by Patrick Lose.
Quilt top made by Shon Jones. Quilted by Lenny Houts.

# Pretty in Pastels

## Required Fabric and Supplies

- $2/_3$ yard lavender for Nine-Patch block
- $5/_8$ yard seafoam (green) for Nine-Patch block
- $2^5/_8$ yards chambray (blue): $5/_8$ yard for quilt top, $1^2/_3$ yards for backing and $1/_3$ yard for binding
- $3/_4$ yard daffodil (yellow) for blocks and border
- Binding and backing: chambray (blue) fabric listed above
- Thin cotton batting: 47" x 47"
- Thread for piecing
- Matching thread for machine quilting

## Cutting Fabrics

Using a rotary cutter, mat, and ruler, cut the following strips selvage to selvage:

**LAVENDER**

Eighteen $1^1/_4$"-wide strips for the Nine-Patch blocks.

**SEAFOAM (GREEN)**

Fifteen $1^1/_4$"-wide strips for the Nine-Patch blocks.

**CHAMBRAY (BLUE)**

Three $7^1/_4$"-wide strips. From the strips, cut forty $2^3/_4$" x $7^1/_4$" rectangles for the sashing strips.

Five $2^1/_8$"-wide strips for binding

Cut and piece backing to measure 47" x 47".

**DAFFODIL (YELLOW)**

Five $2^3/_4$"-wide strips. From the strips cut sixty-four $2^3/_4$" squares for the Double Nine-Patch blocks.

Four $2^3/_4$" x $38^3/_4$" strips for the border.

# Assembling Pieced Blocks

## Nine-Patch block

$2\frac{1}{4}$" finished size

1 Stitch the seafoam (green) and lavender strips together as shown. Press all of the seams toward the seafoam (green) fabric. Cut the strip sets into $1\frac{1}{4}$" units.

$1\frac{1}{4}$" $1\frac{1}{4}$" $1\frac{1}{4}$"

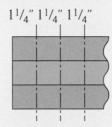

Make 7 strip sets; Cut 218 units

$1\frac{1}{4}$" $1\frac{1}{4}$" $1\frac{1}{4}$"

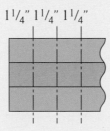

Make 5 strip sets; Cut 109 units

2 Sew the units together to form 109 Nine-Patch blocks. Assemble the blocks so the corners are lavender in color.

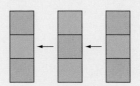

Nine-Patch block

## Double Nine-Patch block

$6\frac{3}{4}$" finished size

3 Stitch daffodil (yellow) $2\frac{3}{4}$" squares to Nine-Patch blocks to form 16 Double Nine-Patch blocks. Press seams toward the daffodil (yellow) squares.

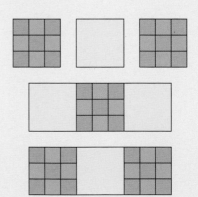

Double Nine-Patch block

## ASSEMBLING THE QUILT TOP

1 Make four rows alternating 5 chambray (blue) sashing strips and 4 Double Nine-Patch blocks. Press seams toward sashing.

2 Make five rows alternating 5 single Nine-Patch blocks and 4 chambray (blue) sashing strips. Press seams toward sashing.

3 Join the rows as shown. Press seams toward sashing rows.

4 Sew a daffodil (yellow) border strip to the top and bottom of the quilt, matching the ends. Press seams toward the border. Sew a Nine-Patch block to both ends of the side border strips. Then sew the side border strips to the quilt sides, matching the Nine-Patch blocks to the top and the bottom borders. Press seams toward the border.

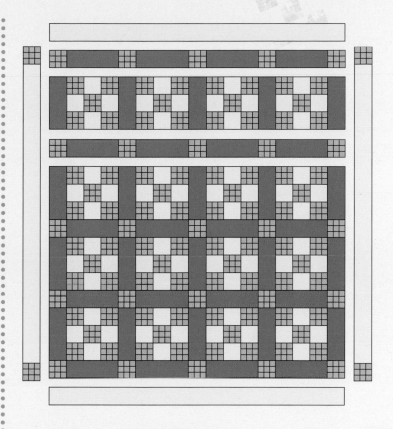

**Quilt Assembly**

## Quilting

1 Sandwich the batting between the quilt top and backing, wrong sides together, smoothing the quilt top from the center. Safety pin all the seams using a ruler to keep the seams straight.

2 Using a walking foot and monofilament thread, stitch-in-the-ditch on the vertical and horizontal seams of each Double Nine-Patch block,

around each Double Nine-Patch block, around each Nine-Patch block in the sashing, and on the seam between the border and the interior of the quilt top.

3 Switch to matching thread. In the daffodil (yellow) squares of the Double Nine-Patch blocks, stitch diagonally from the upper left corner of one daffodil (yellow) square to the lower right corner of the next diagonal daffodil (yellow) square. When all the daffodil (yellow) squares are stitched, rotate the quilt one quarter turn to the left and continue stitching in the same manner. When finished, you will have an X in every daffodil (yellow) square.

4 Switch to matching thread. Starting at the upper chambray corner of the quilt top in the chambray (blue) sashing block, sew a continuous line of stitching to the bottom right corner of the block. Continue for every chambray (blue) sashing block, working down to the lower right corner of the quilt.

5 When all the lines are stitched as above, rotate your quilt one-quarter turn to the left and continue stitching in the same manner. When finished, you will have an X in every chambray (blue) sashing block.

6 In the border, use matching thread and stitch straight lines from each of the Nine-Patch blocks in the sashing to the outside of the border.

Bind your quilt referring to the General Instructions, pages 10-12.

Cheerful Choo-Choo, 1999,
40$\frac{1}{2}$" x 54 $\frac{1}{2}$"
Designed by Patrick Lose.
Quilt top made and quilted
by Lenny Houts.

# Cheerful Choo-Choo

## Required Fabric and Supplies

- $3/4$ yard lime green for Pinwheel blocks and appliqué background panel

- $3/4$ yard blue for Pinwheel blocks, appliqué, and border squares

- $2\,7/8$ yards fuchsia: $2/3$ yard Pinwheel blocks and appliqué, $1/3$ yard for binding, and $1\,7/8$ yards for backing

- 1 yard yellow for Pinwheel blocks, appliqué, sashing, and border

- Binding and backing: fuchsia fabric listed above

- Thin cotton batting: 44" x 58"

- 1 yard fusible adhesive

- Thread for piecing

- Tear away-stabilizer

- Matching thread for machine appliqué and quilting

- Off-white Jeans Stitch™ thread

## Cutting Fabrics

Using a rotary cutter, mat, and ruler, cut the following strips selvage to selvage:

### LIME GREEN

Two $7\,1/4$"-wide strips. From the strips, cut nine $7\,1/4$" squares. Then cut the squares in half diagonally twice for Pinwheel blocks.

One $12\,1/2$" x $36\,1/2$" piece for the appliqué background and panel

### BLUE

Two $7\,1/4$"-wide strips. From the strips, cut nine $7\,1/4$" squares. Then cut the squares in half diagonally twice for Pinwheel blocks.

One $2\,1/2$" x 15" strip. Then cut the strip into six $2\,1/2$"-squares for the border squares.

### FUCHSIA

Two $7\,1/4$"-wide strips. From the strips, cut nine $7\,1/4$" squares. Then cut the squares in half diagonally twice for the Pinwheel blocks.

Five $2\,1/8$"-wide strips. Piece the strips together end-to-end for the binding.

Cut and piece backing to measure 44" x 58".

**YELLOW**

Two $7\frac{1}{4}$"-wide strips. From the strips, cut nine $7\frac{1}{4}$" squares. Then cut the squares in half diagonally twice for the Pinwheel blocks.

Two $2\frac{1}{2}$" x $12\frac{1}{2}$" strips and four $2\frac{1}{2}$" x $36\frac{1}{2}$" strips for the border.

One $2\frac{1}{2}$" x $36\frac{1}{2}$" strip for the sashing.

## Fusible Appliqué Preparation

All appliqué pattern pieces for this project are on pages 93-98. They are printed actual size and reversed for tracing onto fusible adhesive. Join the pieces when tracing as indicated on the pattern.

1 Lay the fusible adhesive, paper side up, over each pattern and use a pencil to trace onto the paper side. Write the pattern number on each piece as you trace.

2 Use paper-cutting scissors to roughly cut all the pieces approximately 1" outside the traced lines.

3 Trim the fusible adhesive to within $\frac{1}{8}$" of the inside edge of the traced pattern before fusing it to the fabric.

4 Following manufacturer's instructions for fusing, fuse the traced pattern onto the wrong side of the fabric (indicated by color).

**Blue:** train (T1–T3, T5, T6 and track)

**Fuchsia:** train (T3, T5, T6, T13–T18)

**Yellow:** train (T4, T7–T12)

5 Cut out the pieces along the traced lines.

6 Transfer any placement and detail stitching lines to the right side of the fabric using a lightbox and a pencil.

## ASSEMBLING THE APPLIQUÉ PANEL

*Note: Place and fuse track onto center panel 1¹/₂" from bottom edge. Then assemble the top section of the quilt, before positioning and fusing the rest of the appliqué.*

1 Sew a 2¹/₂" blue square to each end of two 2¹/₂" x 36¹/₂" border strips and the one sashing strip.

2 Sew the short border side strip to the appliqué background panel. Sew the top border and sashing unit to the panel.

2 When you are satisfied with the placement, fuse the pieces into place, making sure that you smooth the larger pieces as you proceed.

## Zigzag Stitch Appliqué

Use a tear-away stabilizer on the wrong side of the appliqué background fabric. Using matching thread suitable for machine appliqué, zigzag stitch around the appliqué pieces. To zigzag stitch,

## POSITION AND FUSE THE APPLIQUÉ PIECES

1 Referring to the photo or illustration for placement, remove the paper backing and position all appliqué pieces onto the center panel, overlapping some as necessary.

use a long, narrow zigzag stitch. Stitch over the raw edges of the fused appliqué pieces. Work outward from the center and smooth the fabric as you proceed. Tear away the stabilizer when finished.

# Assembling Pieced Blocks

## Pinwheel block

12" finished size

1 Sew together a fuchsia and yellow quarter-square triangle along one short side. Press seams toward the fuchsia triangle. Sew together a blue and lime green quarter-square triangle along one short side. Press seams toward the lime green triangle. Sew the two units together along the long diagonal edge. Press seams toward blue/lime triangles.

2 Sew block units together. Make nine blocks. Press seams open.

## ASSEMBLING THE QUILT TOP

1 Sew three blocks together to make a row. Make three rows together. Press seams open.

2 Sew a border strip to the sides of the quilt top. Press seams toward border. Then sew a bottom border to the bottom of the quilt top. Press seams toward border.

3 Sew the appliqué panel to the top of the quilt top.

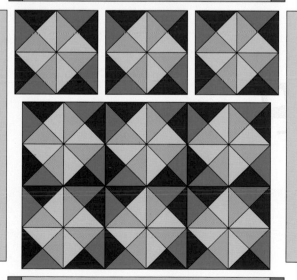

Quilt assembly

## Quilting

1 Sandwich the batting between the top and backing, wrong sides together, smoothing the quilt top from the center. Safety pin all the seams using a ruler to keep the seams straight.

2 Using off-white Jeans Stitch thread and a walking foot, stitch $1/4$" inside each triangle, sashing, border, and border square. (Your local retailer can direct you to Jeans Stitch.) Note: You may need to adjust the tension on your machine with this thread, so test it on a scrap of fabric sandwiched with batting before diving into the project.

3 Using matching thread, stitch next to the zigzag stitching around all the appliqué shapes.

4 Use the off-white Jeans Stitch thread to stitch the smoke coming from the engine's smokestack.

Bind the quilt referring to the General Instructions, pages 10-12.

A Horse of a Different Color, 1999,
28½" x 28½"
Designed by Patrick Lose.
Quilt top made and quilted by Lenny Houts.

# A Horse of a Different Color

## Required Fabric and Supplies

- 1 yard aqua: $3/4$ yard for background and $1/4$ yard for binding
- $1/4$ yard coral for saddle, halter and border
- $1/3$ yard daffodil (yellow) for saddle blanket, halter circles, and border
- $1/4$ yard lilac for spots
- $1^1/4$ yard violet: $1/4$ yard for horse and 1 yard for backing
- Backing: violet fabric listed above
- Binding: aqua fabric listed above
- Thin cotton batting: 33" x 33" for entire quilt and 22" x 22" for Rocking Horse appliqué
- 1 yard lightweight fusible adhesive
- Thread for piecing
- Tear-away stabilizer
- Matching thread for machine appliqué and quilting

## Cutting Fabrics

Using a rotary cutter, mat, and ruler, cut the following strips selvage to selvage:

**AQUA**

One $2^1/2$" x 12" strip. From the strip, cut four $2^1/2$" squares for the border corners.

One $24^1/2$" x $24^1/2$" piece for the appliqué background panel

Three $2^1/8$"-wide strips. Piece the strips together end-to-end for the binding.

**CORAL**

Two $2^7/8$"-wide strips. From the strips, cut twenty-four $2^7/8$" squares. Then cut the squares in half diagonally for the border.

**DAFFODIL (YELLOW)**

Two $2^7/8$"-wide strips. From the strips, cut twenty-four $2^7/8$" squares. Then cut the squares in half diagonally for the border.

**VIOLET**

Cut backing to measure 33" x 33".

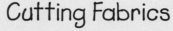

## Fusible Appliqué Preparation

All appliqué pattern pieces for this project are on pages 99-105. They are printed actual size and reversed for tracing onto fusible adhesive. Join the pieces when tracing as indicated on the pattern.

1 Lay the fusible adhesive, paper side up, over each pattern and use a pencil to trace onto the paper side. Write the pattern number on each piece as you trace.

2 Use paper-cutting scissors to roughly cut all the pieces approximately 1" outside the traced lines.

3 Trim the fusible adhesive to within $1/8$" of the inside edge of the traced pattern before fusing it to the fabric.

4 Following manufacturer's instructions for fusing, fuse the traced pattern onto the wrong side of the fabric (indicated by color).

**Coral:** saddle (H1);

   halter (H2)

**Daffodil (yellow):** star (H3);

   saddle blanket (H4);

   circles on halter (H5)

**Lilac:** ear (H6);

   eye (H7);

   nostril (H8);

   spots (H9–H14);

   rocker (H15)

**Fuchsia:** horse (H16-H21)

5 Cut out the pieces along the traced lines.

6 Transfer any placement to the right side of the fabric using a lightbox and a pencil. Transfer detail quilting lines using a Chaco-Liner.

## ASSEMBLING THE QUILT TOP

*Note: With this quilt, you will first need to assemble the quilt top, before positioning and fusing the appliqué.*

1 For the border, stitch 48 half-square triangle units of coral and daffodil (yellow). Press seams toward coral triangles.

2 Sew 12 half-square triangle units together for each of the four borders. Press seams toward the coral triangle.

3 Sew a border strip to each side of the quilt top. Press seams toward the quilt.

4 Sew a corner square to each end of the top and bottom borders. Press seam toward the square. Then sew the top and bottom borders to the quilt top. Press seam toward the quilt.

Quilt assembly

## POSITION AND FUSE THE APPLIQUÉ PIECES

1 Referring to the photo or illustration for placement, remove the paper backing and position all appliqué pieces onto the center panel, overlapping some as necessary.

2 When you are satisfied with the placement, fuse the pieces into place, making sure that you smooth the larger pieces as you proceed.

### Zigzag Stitch Appliqué

Sandwich the quilt top, the 22" x 22" piece of batting, and tear-away stabilizer. With matching thread suitable for machine appliqué, zigzag stitch around all raw edges of the appliqué pieces. To zigzag stitch, use a long, narrow zigzag stitch. Work outward from the center and smooth the fabric as you proceed. Tear away the stabilizer. Cut away the batting around the outside of the Rocking Horse and on the inside between the legs.

# Quilting

1 Sandwich the 33" x 33" piece batting between the top and backing, wrong sides together, smoothing out from the center. Safety pin using a ruler around the outside border to ensure that it is straight.

2 Using matching threads and a walking foot, stitch around each appliqué shape of the Rocking Horse outside of the zigzag stitching. This will give a trapunto look to the quilt.

3 Using matching thread, straight stitch the details.

4 Drop the feed dogs of your sewing machine. Using a darning foot, stipple the background with matching thread.

Stippling quilting lines

5 With a walking foot, stitch-in-the-ditch around the inside of the border.

6 With matching thread, stitch-in-the-ditch around each triangle in the border.

Bind the quilt referring to the General Instructions, pages 10-12.

Hugs and Kisses, 1999,
36½" x 48½"
Designed by Patrick Lose.
Quilt top made and quilted by Lenny Houts.

# Hugs and Kisses

# Required Fabric and Supplies

- $1/4$ yard each of seventeen assorted coordinating fabrics
- $1/3$ yard coordinating fabric for flange accent
- $1/2$ yard coordinating fabric for border
- $1^1/2$ yards coordinating fabric for backing
- $1/3$ yard coordinating fabric for binding
- Binding and backing: coordinating fabrics listed above
- Thin cotton batting: 41" x 53"
- $3/4$ yard lightweight fusible adhesive
- Thread for piecing
- Tear-away stabilizer
- Matching thread for machine appliqué and quilting

# Cutting Fabrics

Using a rotary cutter, mat, and ruler, cut the following blocks from the assorted fabrics:

Three $6^1/2$" x $12^1/2$" blocks for heart appliqué backgrounds

Twelve $6^1/2$" x $6^1/2$" blocks for star, hug, and kiss appliqué backgrounds

Eleven $6^1/2$" x $6^1/2$" blocks

Two $3^1/2$" blocks each of twelve different fabrics for Four-Patch blocks.

Cut four $3/4$"-wide strips for flange accent insert. Cut two $30^1/2$" lengths for the top and bottom inserts, and two $42^1/2$" lengths for the side inserts.

Cut four $3^1/2$"-wide strips. Cut two $42^1/2$" lengths for the side border. Cut two $36^1/2$" lengths for the top and bottom border from remaining two strips.

Cut backing to measure 40" x 52"

Five $2^1/8$"-wide strips for the binding. Piece the strips together end-to-end.

# Fusible Appliqué Preparation

All appliqué pattern pieces for this project are on pages 106-109. They are printed actual size and reversed for tracing onto fusible adhesive.

1 Lay the fusible adhesive, paper side up, over each pattern and use a pencil to trace onto the paper side. Write the pattern number on each piece as you trace.

2 Use paper-cutting scissors to roughly cut all the pieces approximately 1" outside the traced lines.

3 Trim the fusible adhesive to within $1/_8$" of the inside edge of the traced pattern before fusing it to the fabric.

4 Following manufacturer's instructions for fusing, fuse the traced pattern onto the wrong side of the fabric (indicated by color).

Assorted fabrics: small heart (xo3);

medium heart (xo4);

large heart (xo5);

small star (xo1);

medium star (xo2);

o for hug (xo7);

x for kiss (xo6)

5 Cut out the pieces along the traced lines.

## POSITION AND FUSE THE APPLIQUÉ PIECES

1 Referring to the photo or illustration for placement, remove the paper backing and position all appliqué pieces onto their respective backgrounds.

2 When you are satisfied with the placement, fuse the pieces into place, making sure that you smooth the larger pieces as you proceed.

## Zigzag Stitch Appliqué

Use a tear-away stabilizer on the wrong side of the background fabrics. With matching thread suitable for machine appliqué, zigzag stitch around the appliqué pieces. To zigzag stitch, use a long, narrow zigzag stitch. Stitch over the raw edges of the fused appliqué pieces. When the zigzag stitching is complete, tear away all the stabilizer.

## Assembling Pieced Blocks

### Four-Patch Block

6" finished size

1 Stitch together two coordinating sets of the 3 1/2" squares, alternating the same color block on the opposite corners of the Four-Patch block. To construct each block, follow the piecing sequence below. Press seams toward the darker color square. Make six blocks.

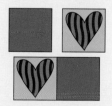

**ASSEMBLING THE QUILT TOP**

2 Using the illustration as a guide, sew the blocks together in vertical rows. Press seams of alternate rows in opposite directions. Then sew the rows together as shown. Press seams in one direction.

3 For the accent flange inserts, press the 3/4"-wide strips in half length wise, wrong sides together. Match raw edges to quilt top and sew to top and bottom of the quilt. Repeat for the sides of the quilt.

4 Sew the border side strips on the quilt top. Press seams toward border. Then add the top and bottom borders. Press seams toward the border.

Quilt assembly

## Quilting

**1** Sandwich the batting between the quilt top and backing, wrong sides together, smoothing the quilt top from the center. Safety pin all the seams using a ruler to keep the seams straight.

**2** With monofilament thread and a walking foot, stitch-in-the-ditch around all the squares.

**3** Continue with the walking foot and switch to matching threads, stitching $1/8$" from zigzag stitching around the hearts, stars, Xs and Os.

**4** Refer to the quilt photo and illustration for quilting designs used in all the squares without a motif. Use a straight stitch and a walking foot. In each of the Four-Patch blocks, I stitched-in-the-ditch. Sometimes I stitched diagonally from corner to corner in two or four of the squares of the Four-Patch block. In the blocks of striped fabric, I chose to quilt random stripes. In the patchwork print blocks, I chose one or more shapes to quilt. Your fabric choices will dictate how you decide to quilt the squares.

Bind the quilt referring to the General Instructions, pages 10-12.

# Patterns

————————— Cutting line

— — — — — Overlap lines

- - - - - - - Appliqué placement

-------------- Quilting lines

—·—·—·— Connection lines

|||||||||||||||||||||| Detail stitching

Project on Page 14

# Rub A Dub Dub

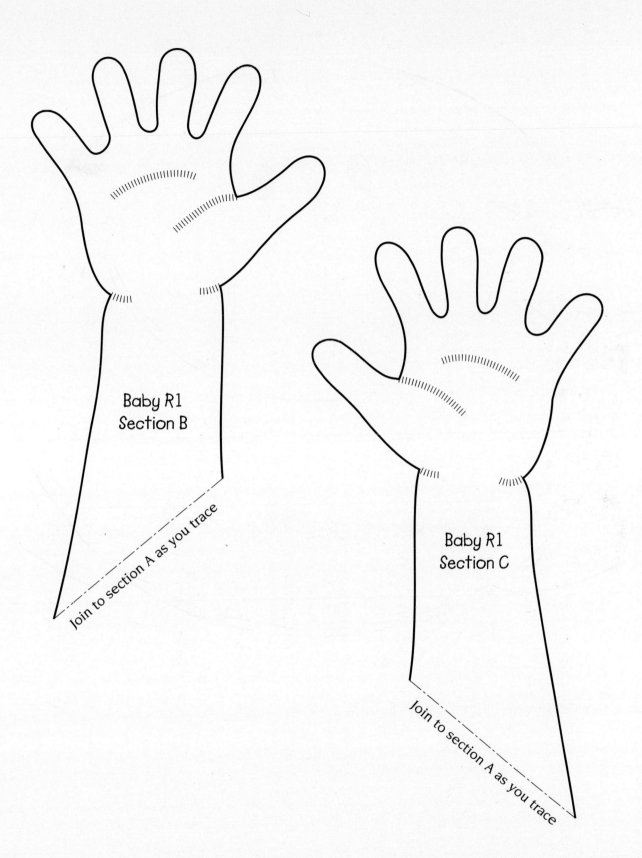

Baby R1
Section B

Join to section A as you trace

Baby R1
Section C

Join to section A as you trace

Baby R1
Section A

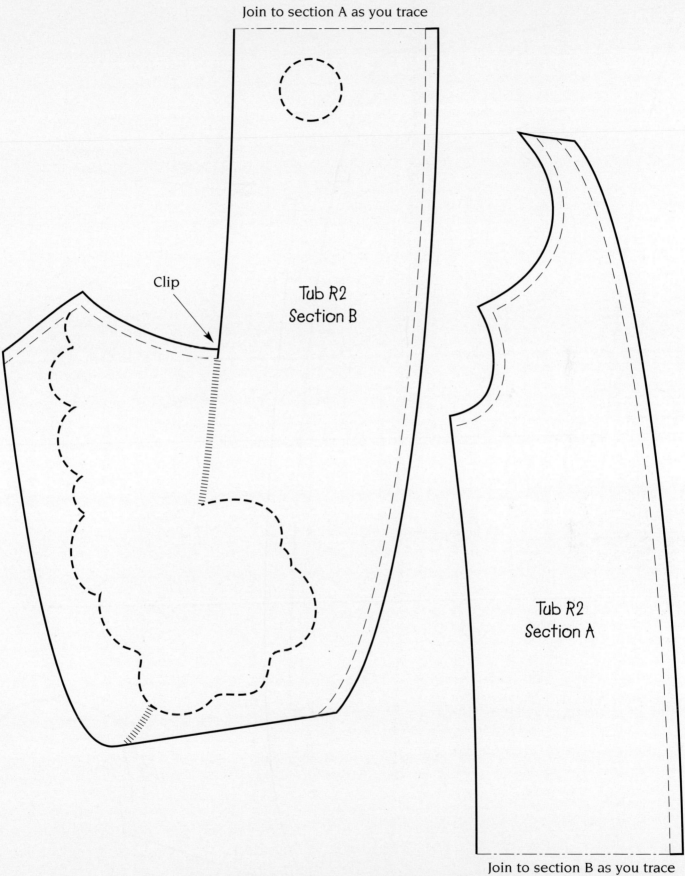

Join to section A as you trace

Clip

Tub R2
Section B

Tub R2
Section A

Join to section B as you trace

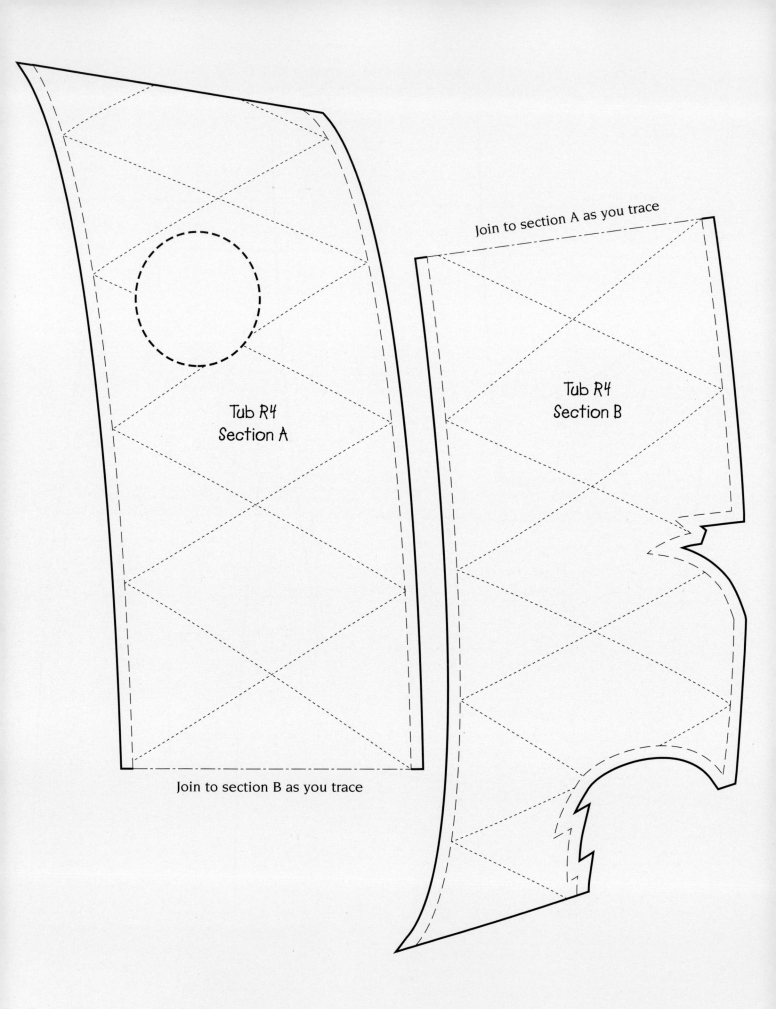

Join to section A as you trace

Tub R4
Section A

Tub R4
Section B

Join to section B as you trace

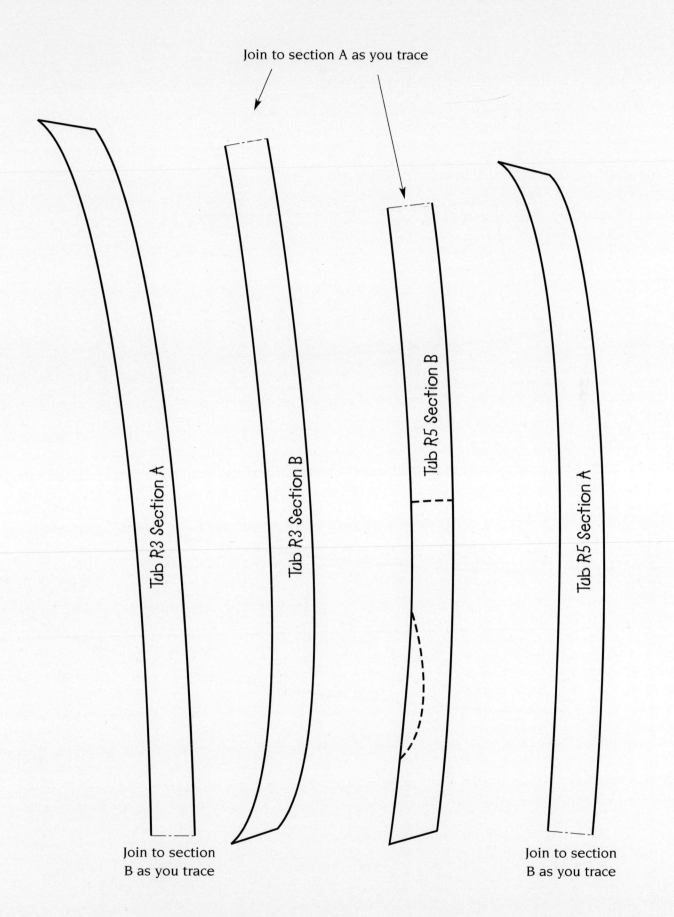

Join to section A as you trace

Tub R3 Section A

Tub R3 Section B

Tub R5 Section B

Tub R5 Section A

Join to section
B as you trace

Join to section
B as you trace

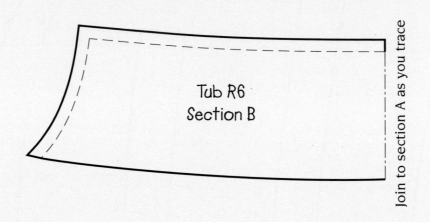

Tub R6
Section B

Join to section A as you trace

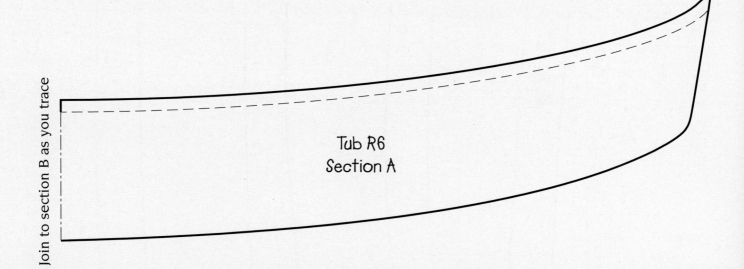

Tub R6
Section A

Join to section B as you trace

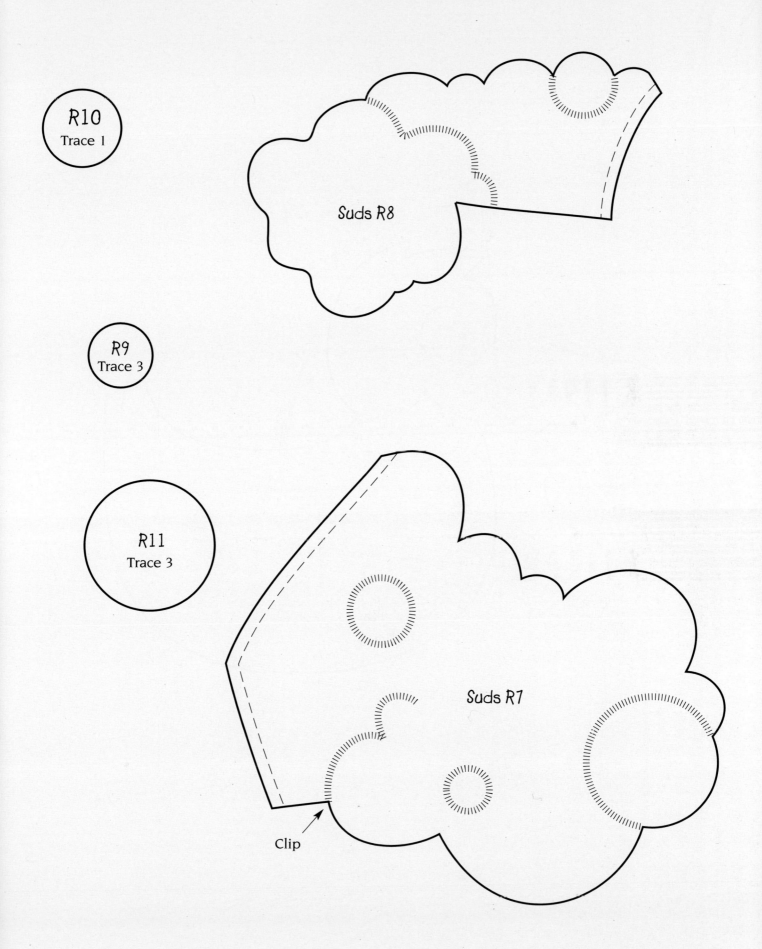

R10
Trace 1

Suds R8

R9
Trace 3

R11
Trace 3

Suds R7

Clip

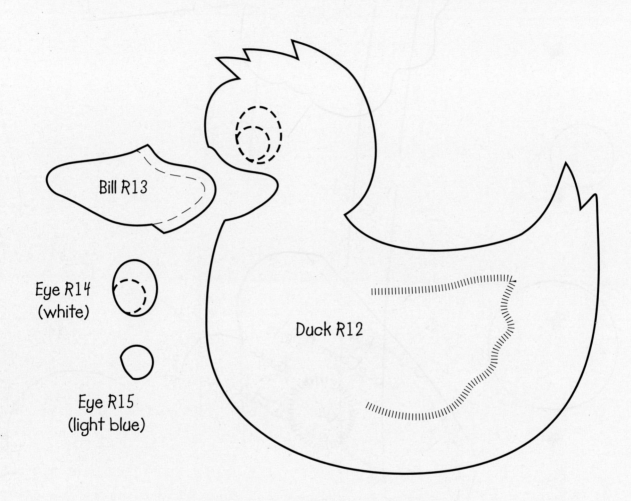

Bill R13

Eye R14
(white)

Eye R15
(light blue)

Duck R12

# Wish Upon A Star

Project on Page 19

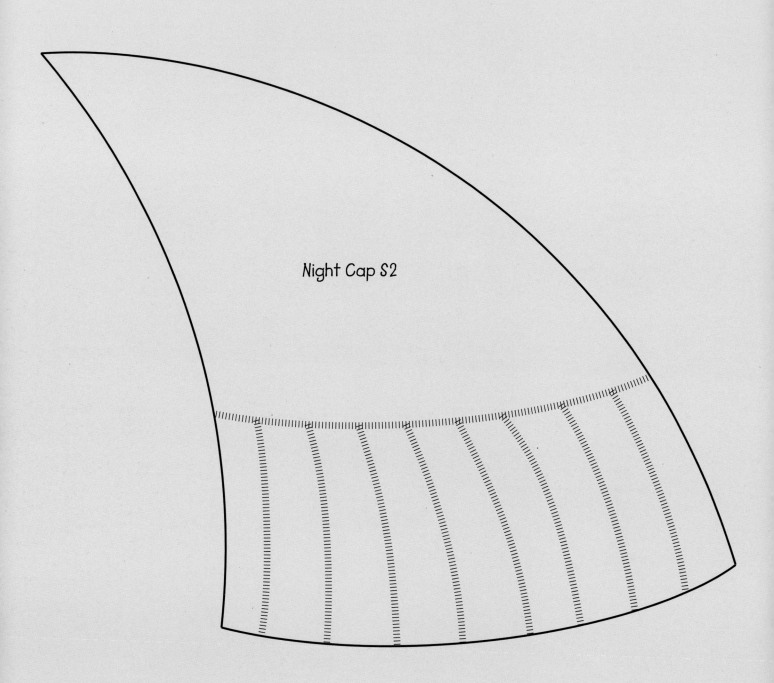

Night Cap S2

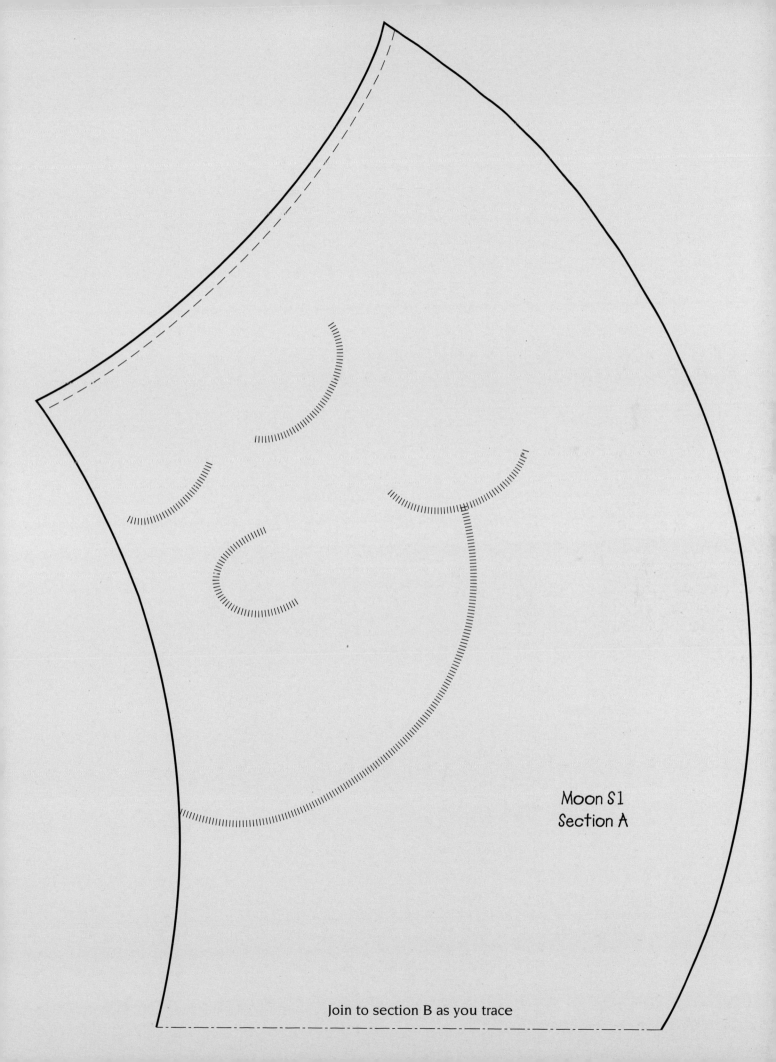

Moon S1
Section A

Join to section B as you trace

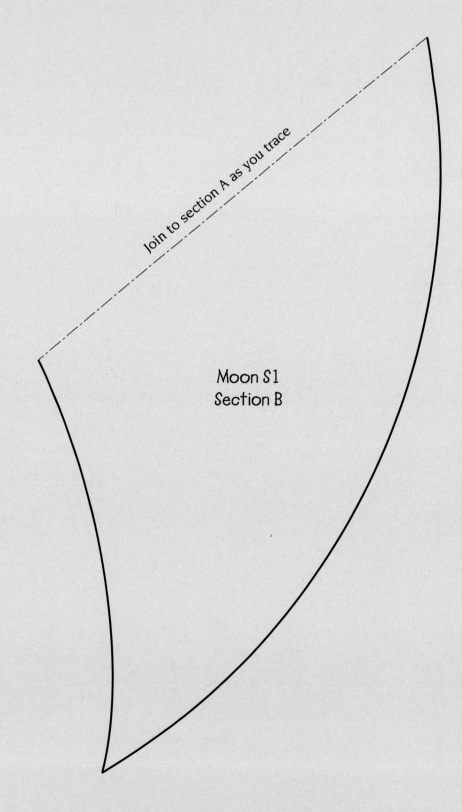

Join to section A as you trace

Moon S1
Section B

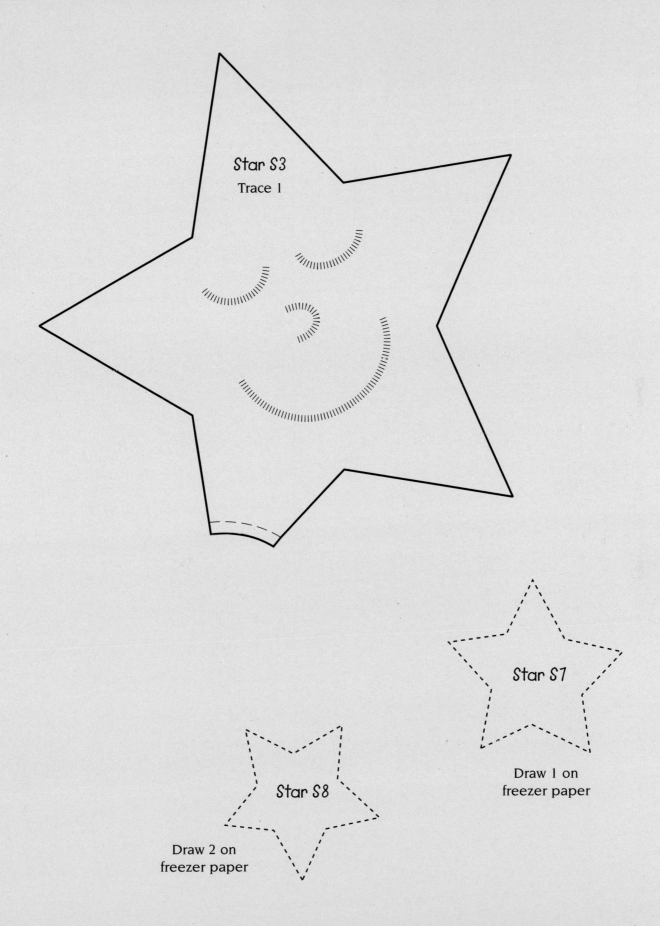

Star S3

Trace 1

Star S7

Draw 1 on freezer paper

Star S8

Draw 2 on freezer paper

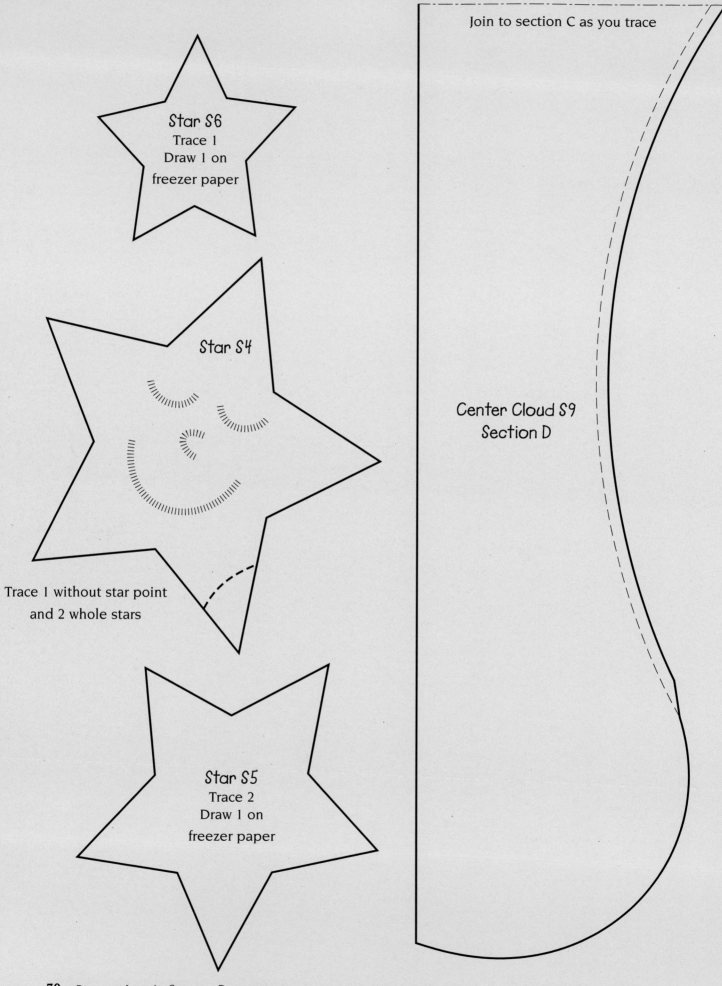

Star S6
Trace 1
Draw 1 on
freezer paper

Join to section C as you trace

Star S4

Center Cloud S9
Section D

Trace 1 without star point
and 2 whole stars

Star S5
Trace 2
Draw 1 on
freezer paper

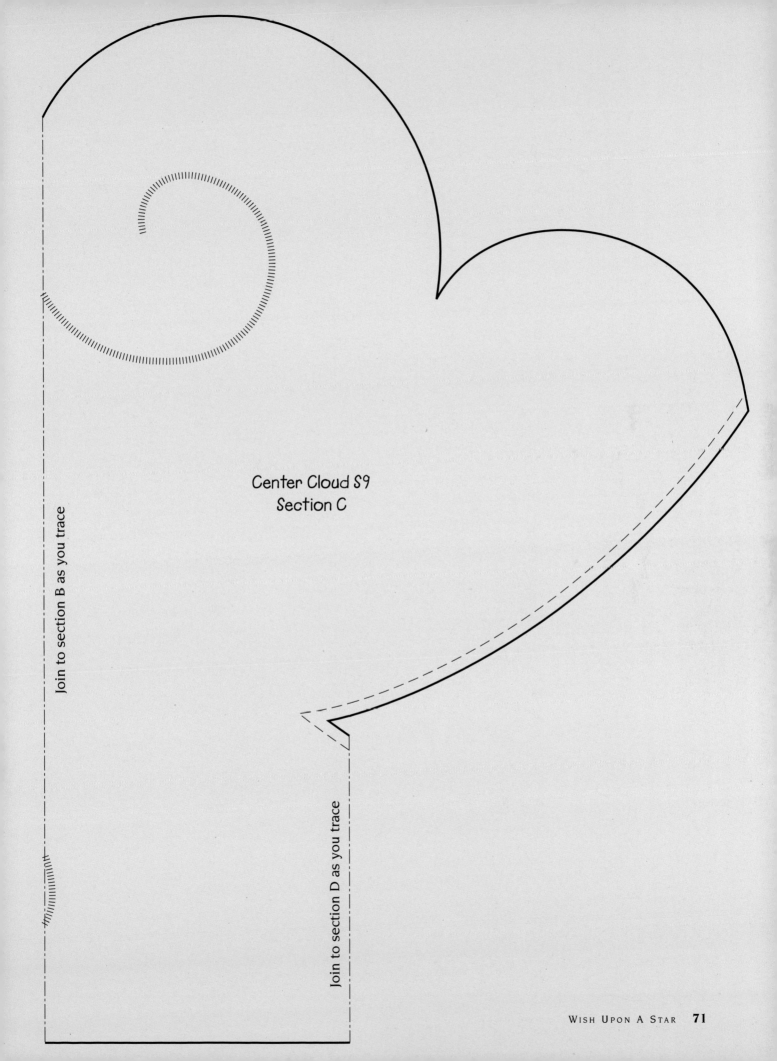

Center Cloud S9
Section C

Join to section B as you trace

Join to section D as you trace

Center Cloud S9
Section B

Join to section A as you trace

Join to section C as you trace

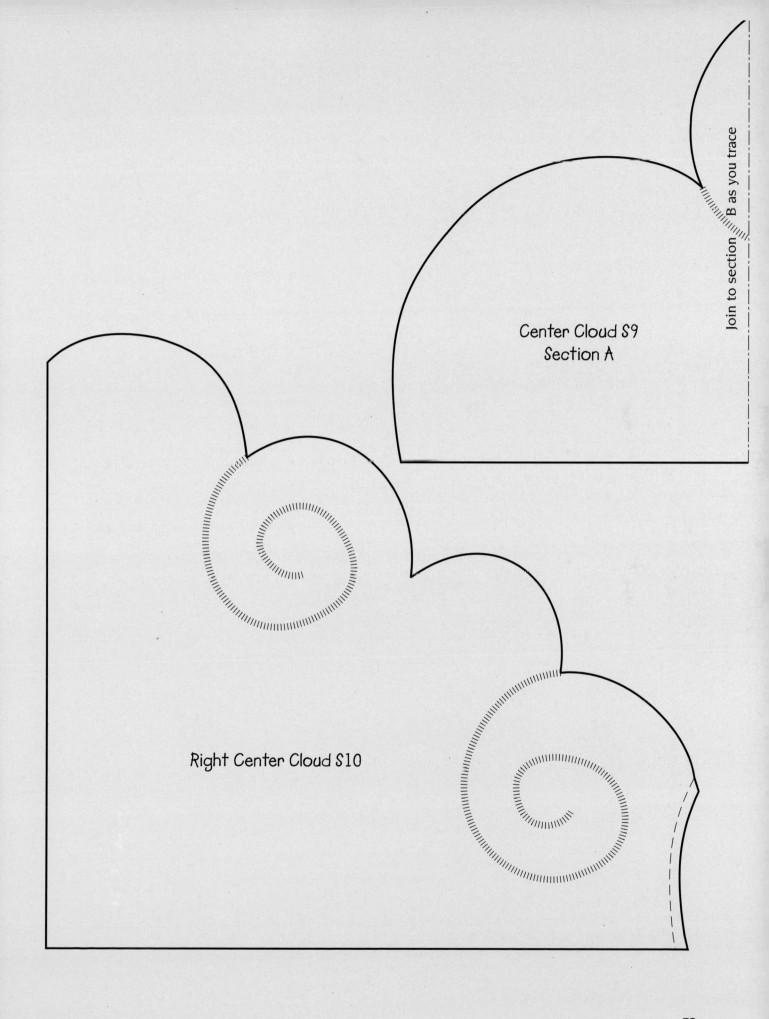

Center Cloud S9
Section A

Join to section B as you trace

Right Center Cloud S10

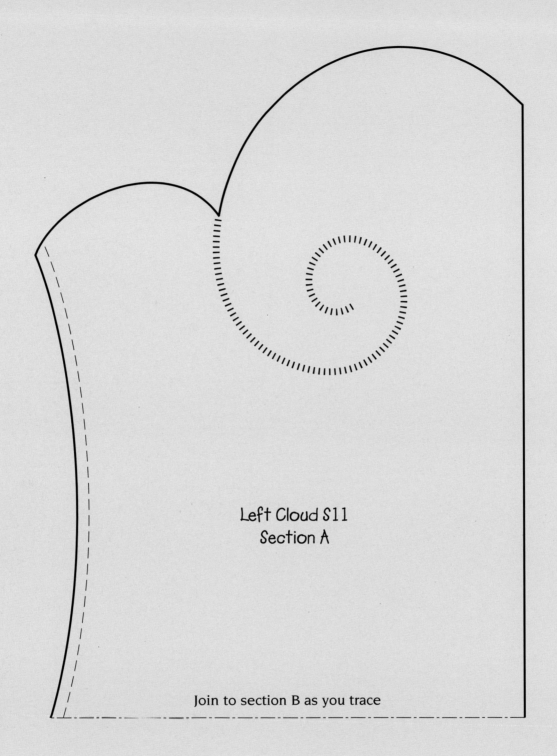

Left Cloud S11
Section A

Join to section B as you trace

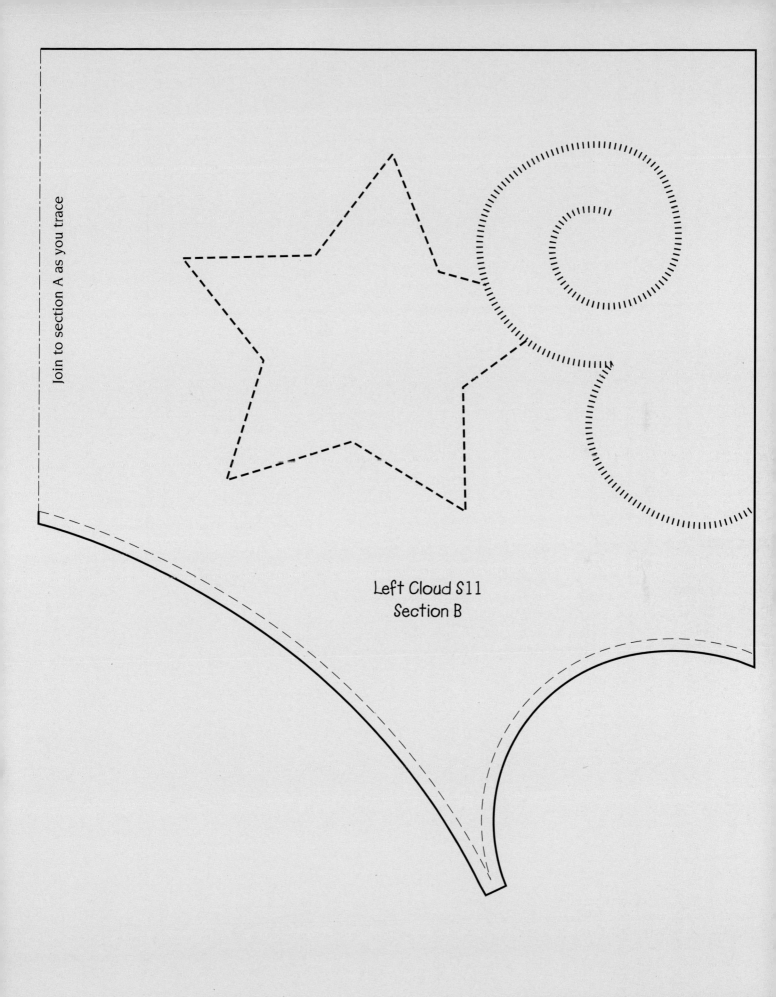

Join to section A as you trace

Left Cloud S11
Section B

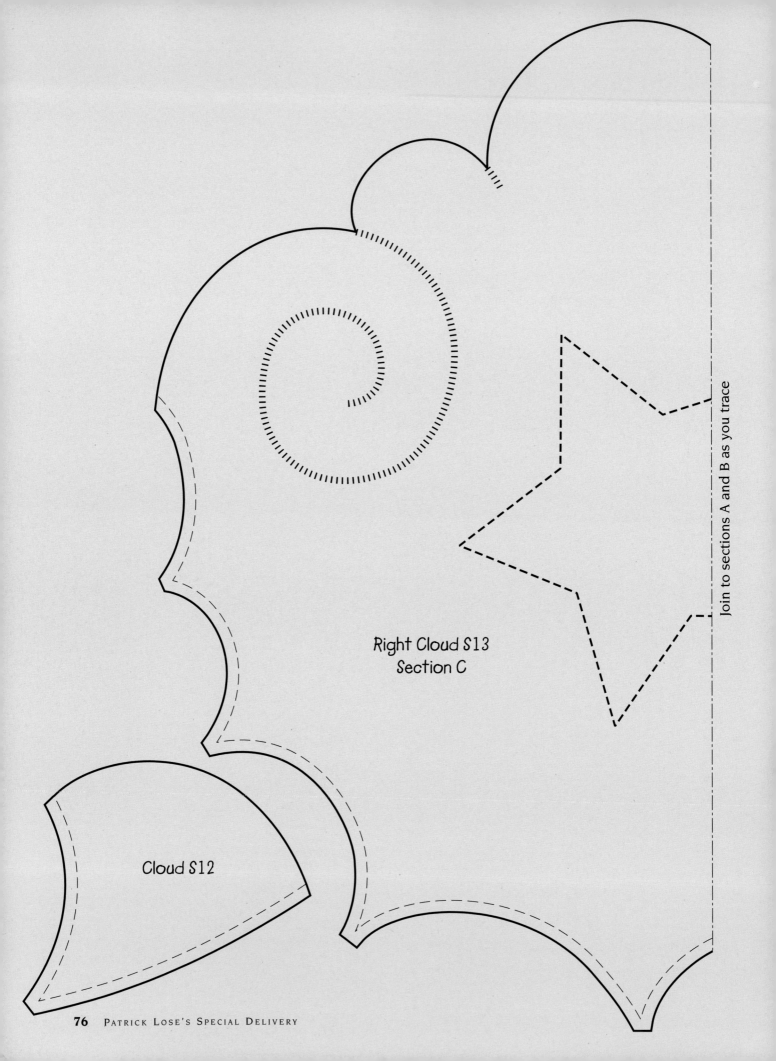

Right Cloud S13
Section C

Cloud S12

Join to sections A and B as you trace

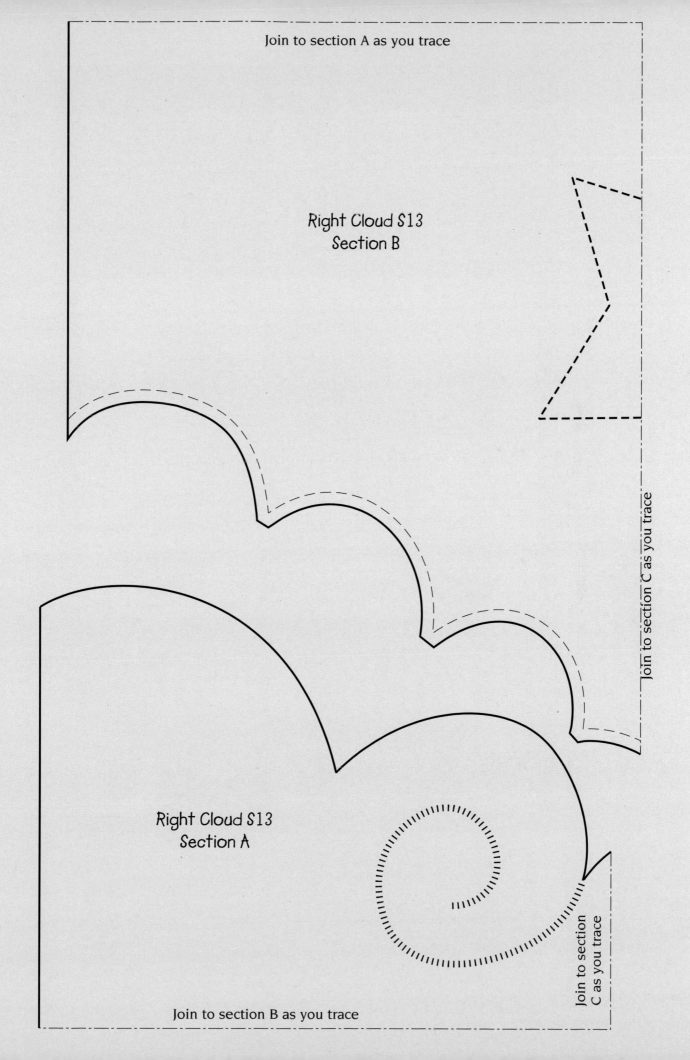

Project on Page 29

# I Love You This Much!

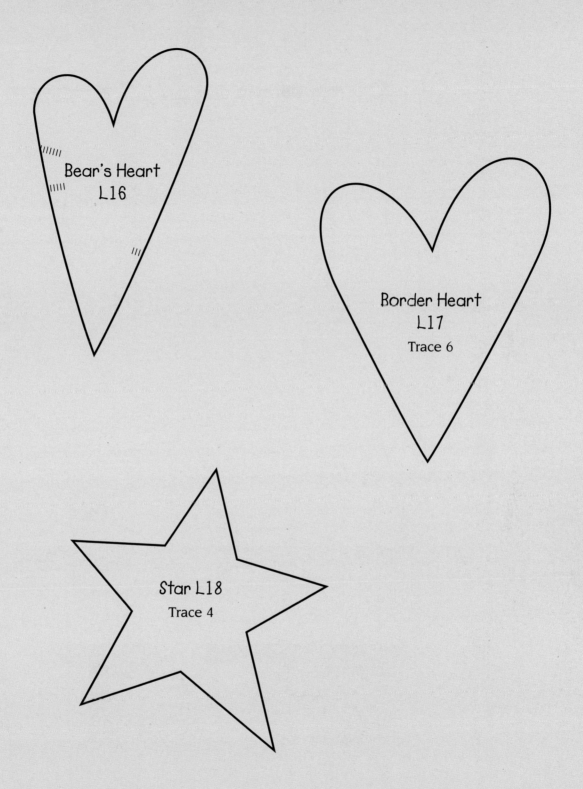

Bear's Heart
L16

Border Heart
L17
Trace 6

Star L18
Trace 4

Trace 2

Trace 2

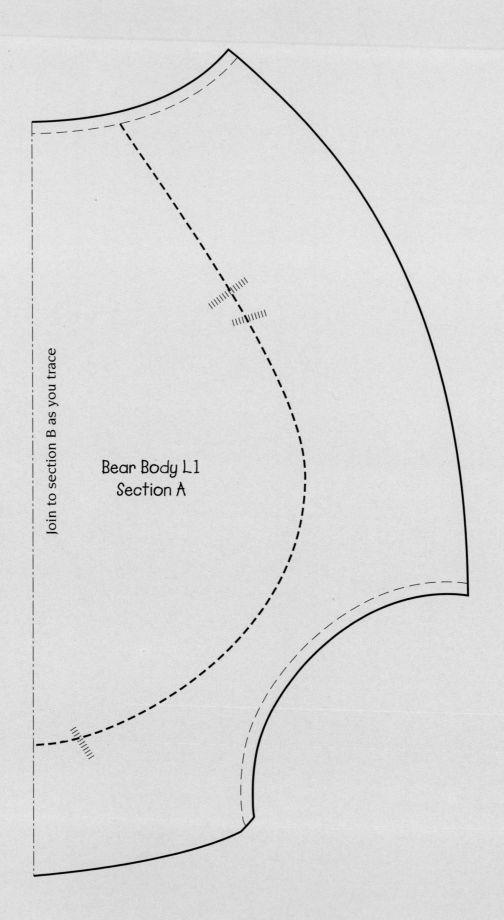

Join to section B as you trace

Bear Body L1
Section A

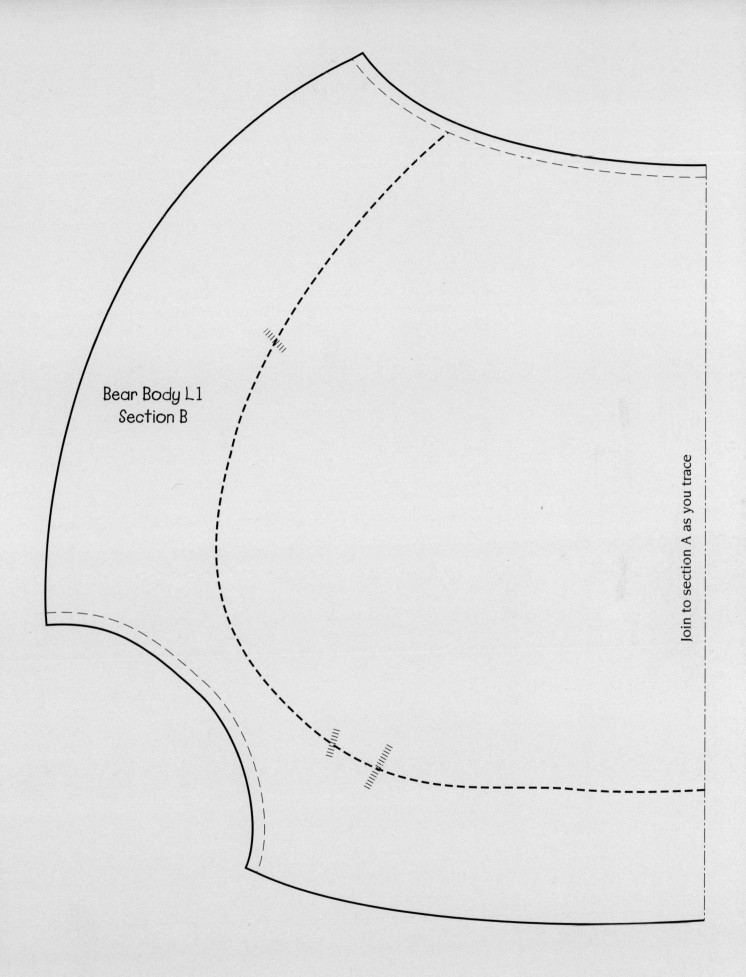

Bear Body L1
Section B

Join to section A as you trace

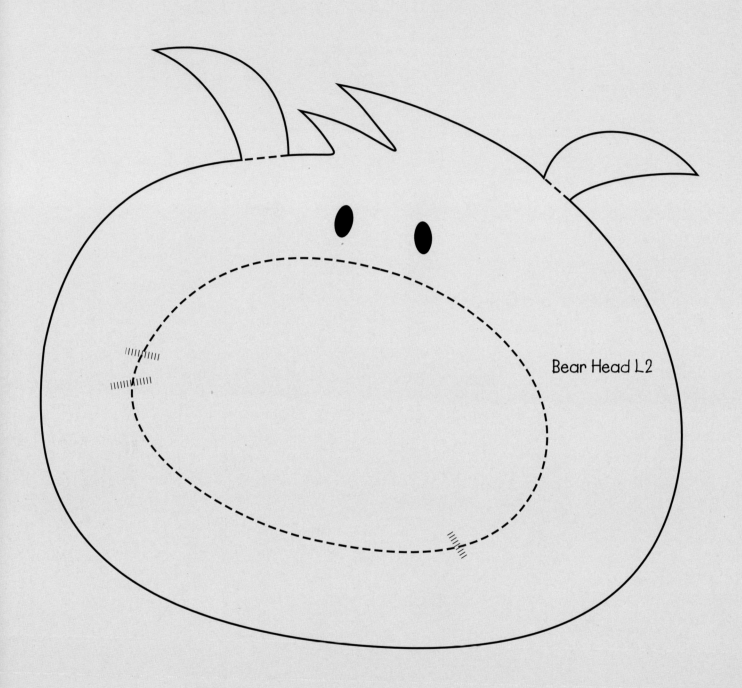

Bear Head L2

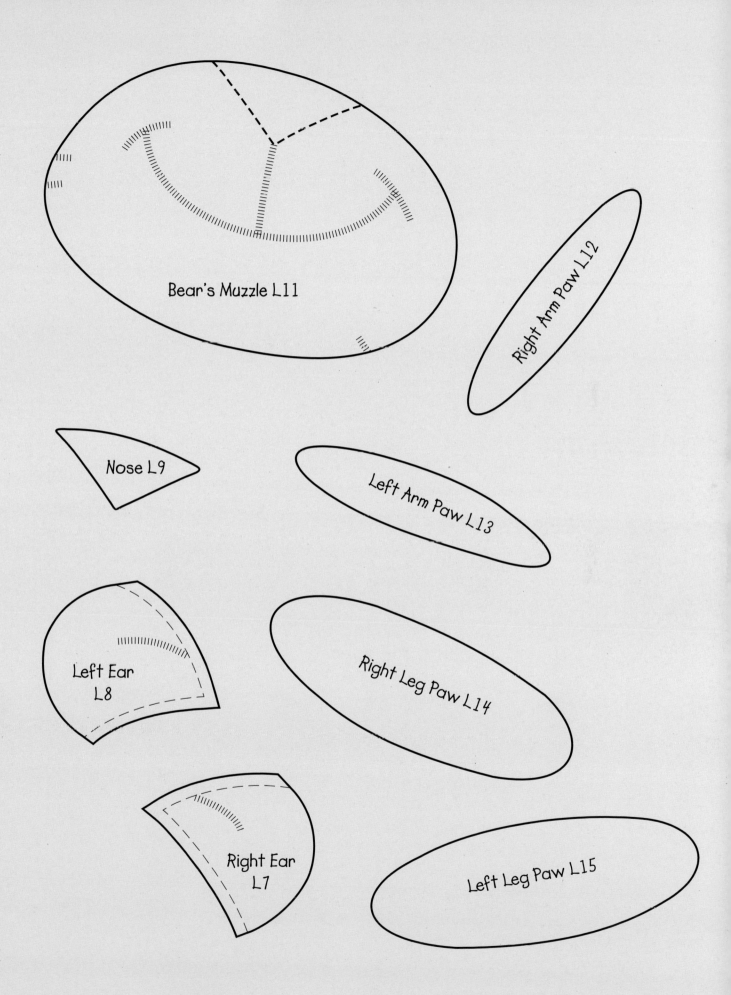

Bear's Muzzle L11

Right Arm Paw L12

Nose L9

Left Arm Paw L13

Left Ear L8

Right Leg Paw L14

Right Ear L7

Left Leg Paw L15

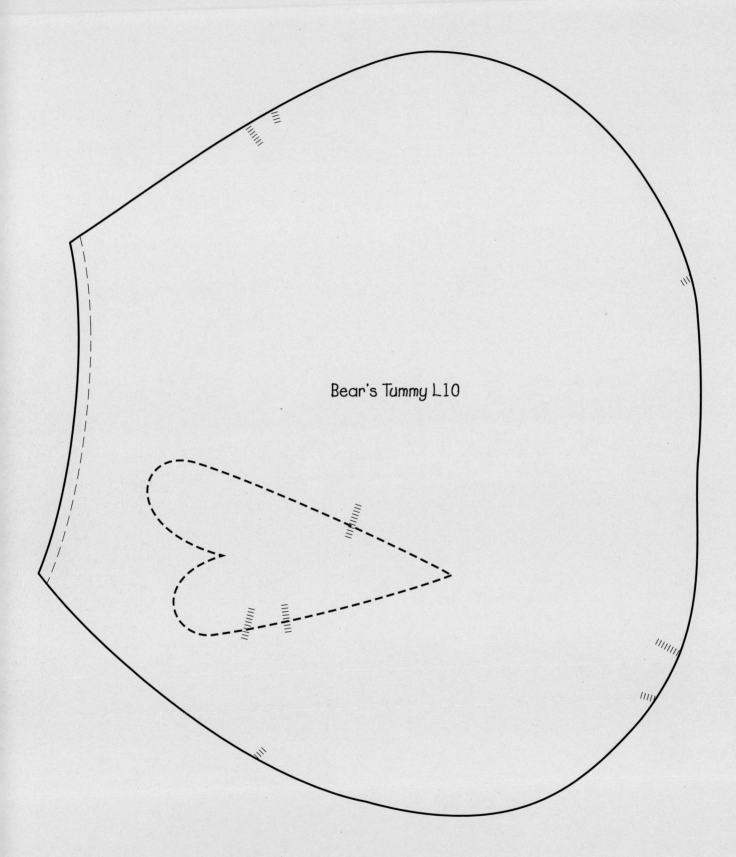

Bear's Tummy L10

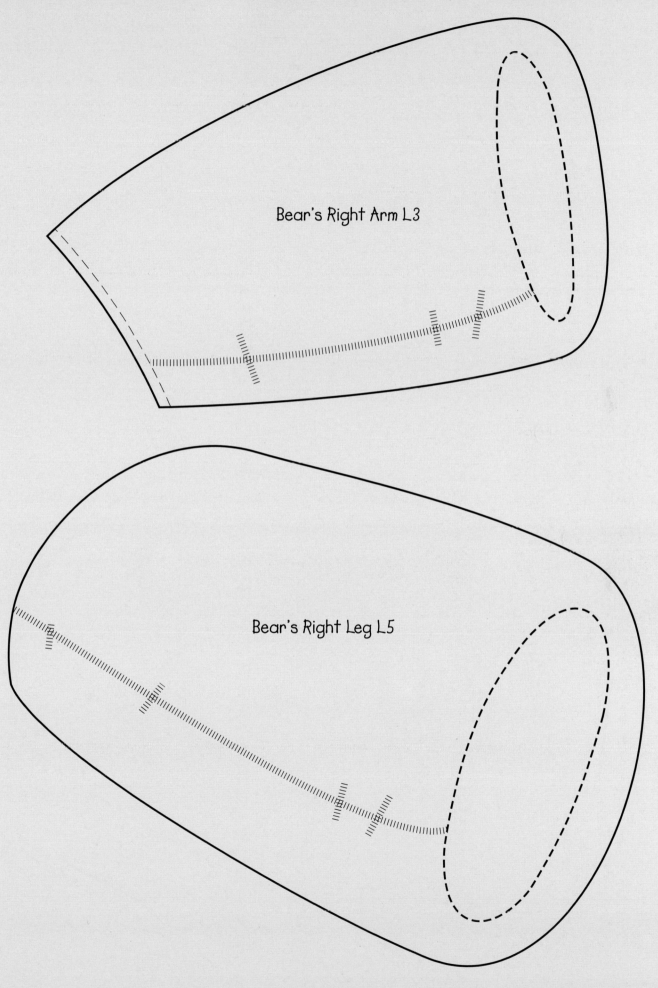

Bear's Right Arm L3

Bear's Right Leg L5

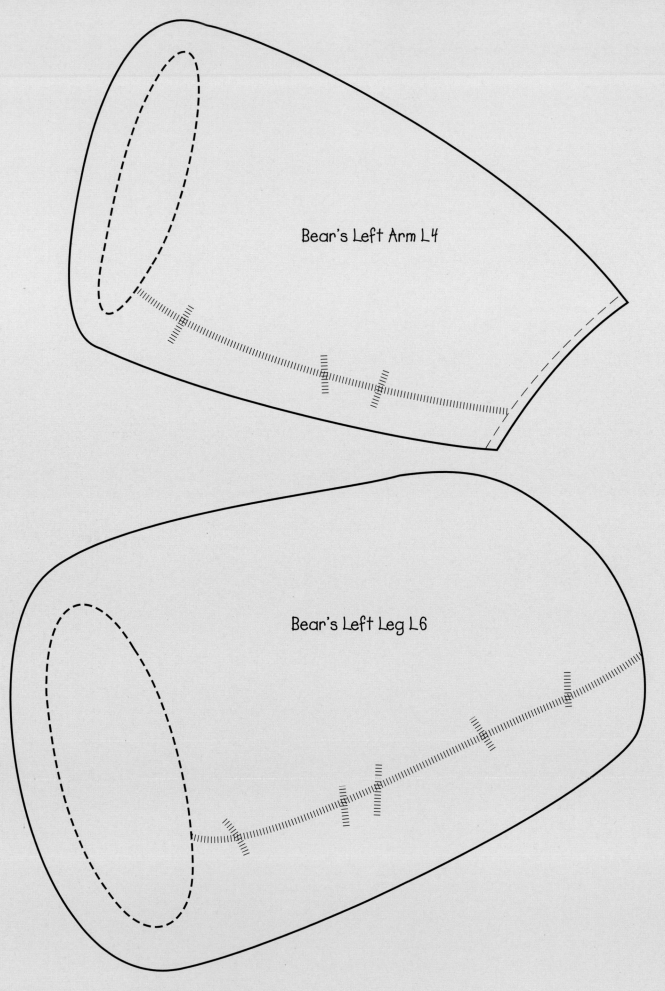

Bear's Left Arm L4

Bear's Left Leg L6

# Cheerful Choo-Choo

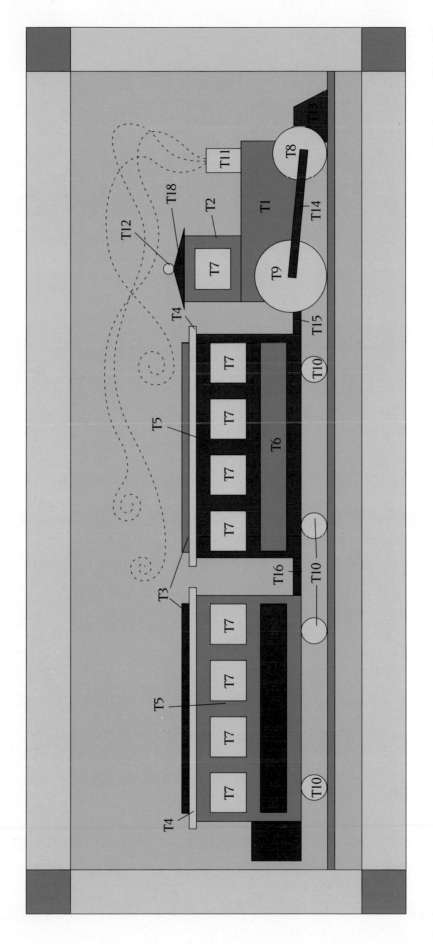

Project on Page 39

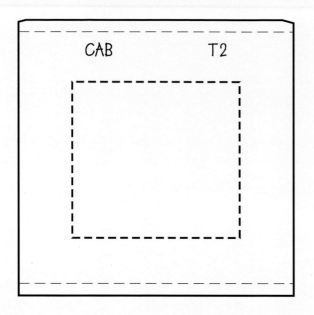

CAB    T2

Window T7
Trace 9

For the train track, cut a strip $3/8$" - wide $36\frac{1}{2}$" long from fusible adhesive. Fuse to blue fabric.

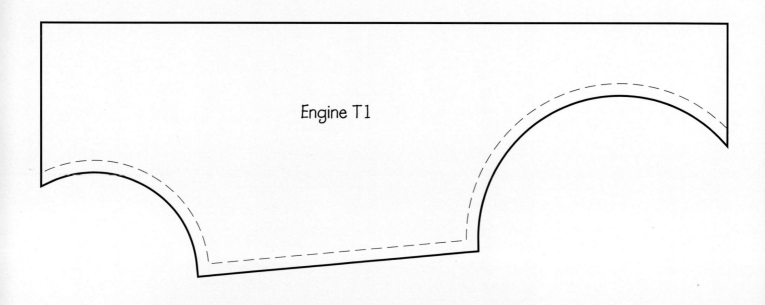

Engine T1

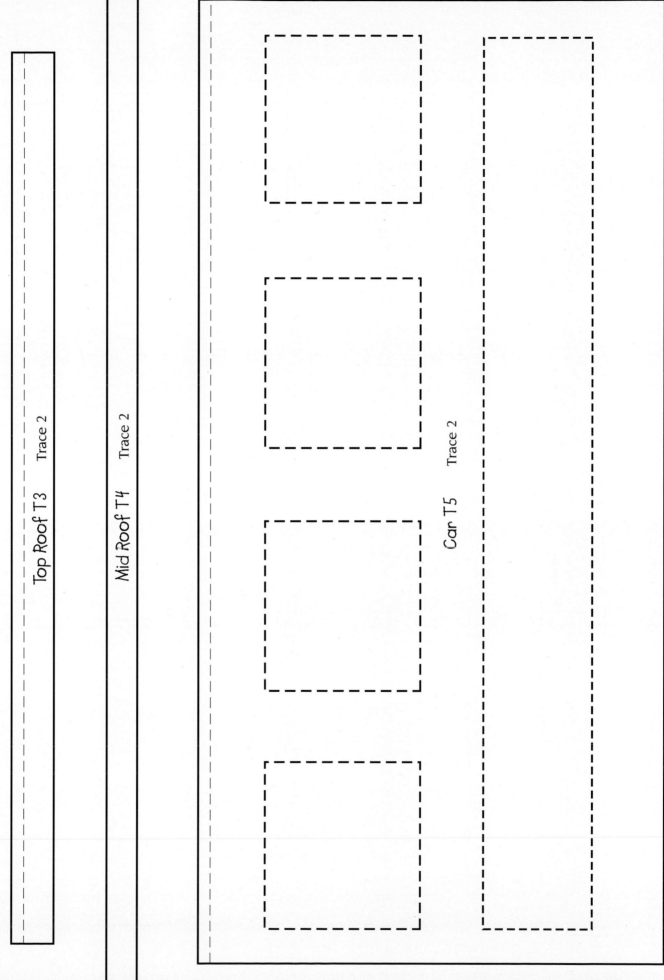

Top Roof T3    Trace 2

Mid Roof T4    Trace 2

Car T5    Trace 2

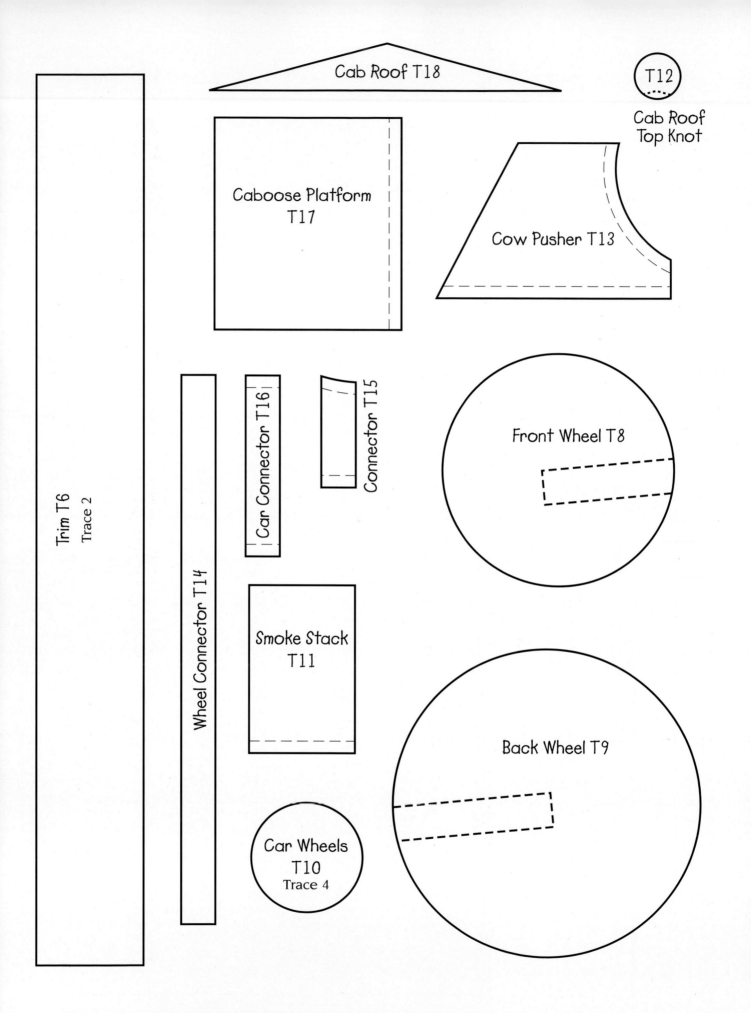

Cab Roof T18

T12
Cab Roof
Top Knot

Caboose Platform
T17

Cow Pusher T13

Trim T6
Trace 2

Wheel Connector T14

Car Connector T16

Connector T15

Front Wheel T8

Smoke Stack
T11

Car Wheels
T10
Trace 4

Back Wheel T9

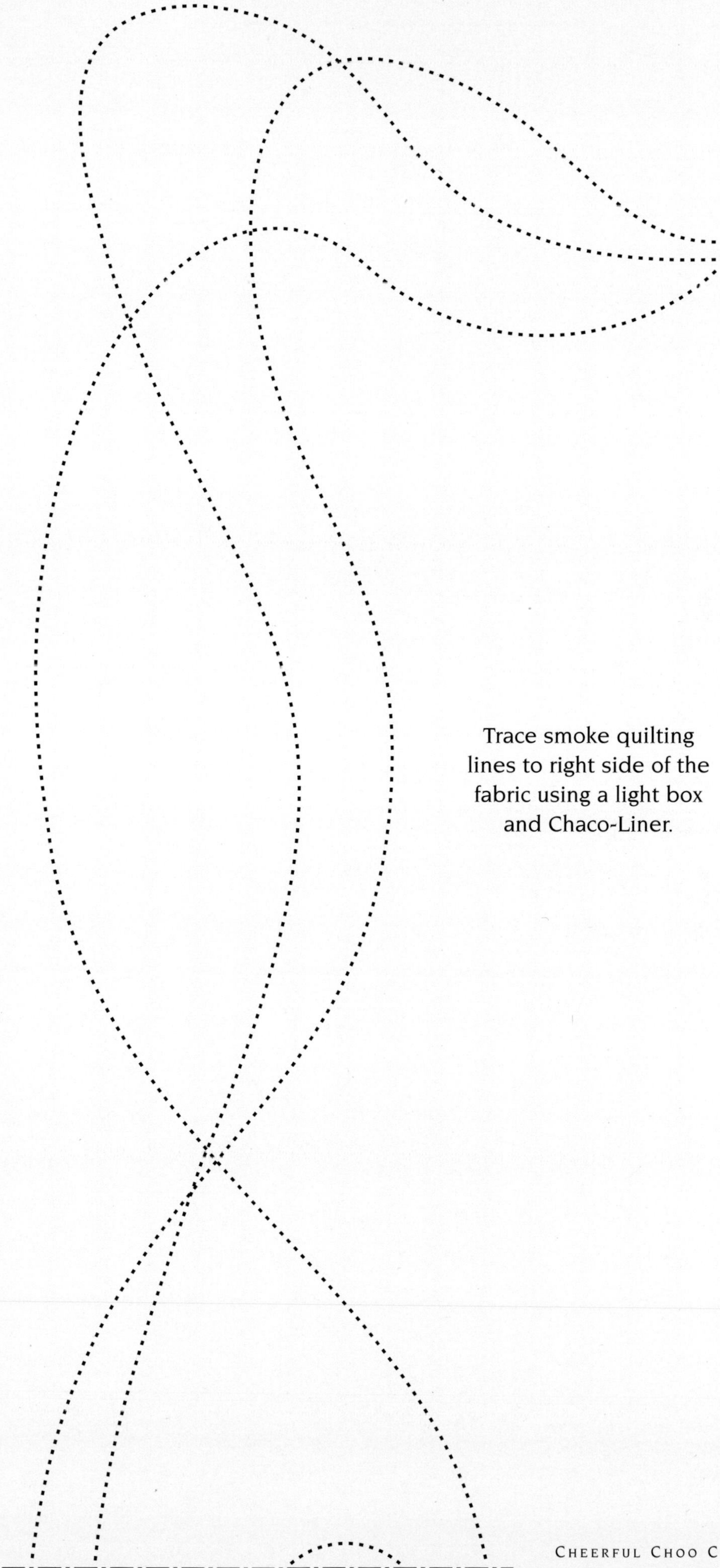

Trace smoke quilting
lines to right side of the
fabric using a light box
and Chaco-Liner.

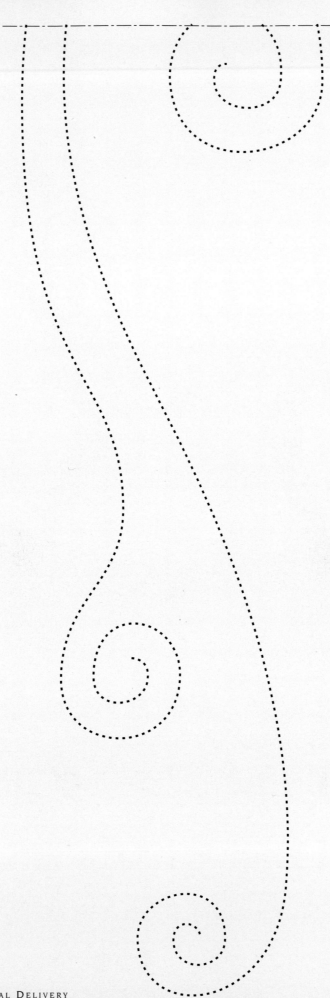

Project on Page 45

# A Horse of a Different Color

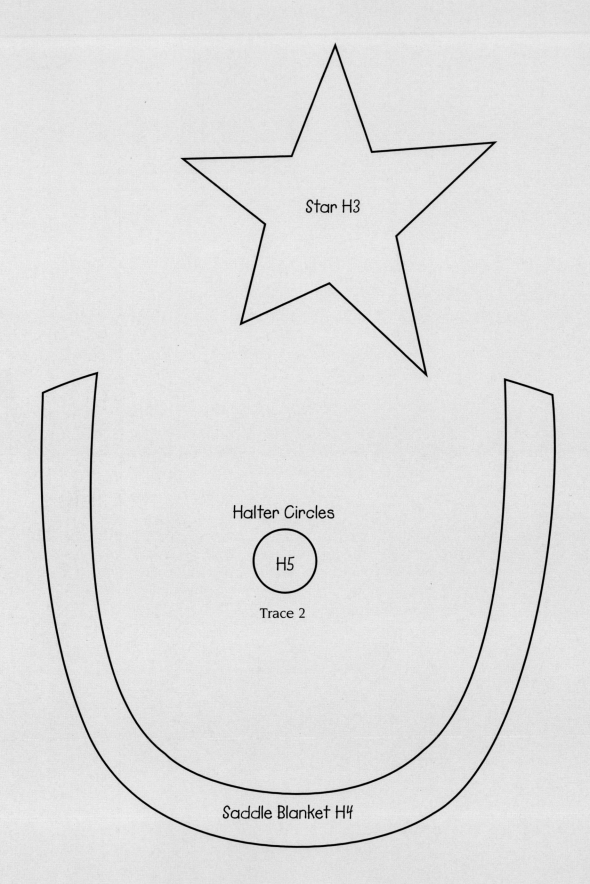

Star H3

Halter Circles

H5

Trace 2

Saddle Blanket H4

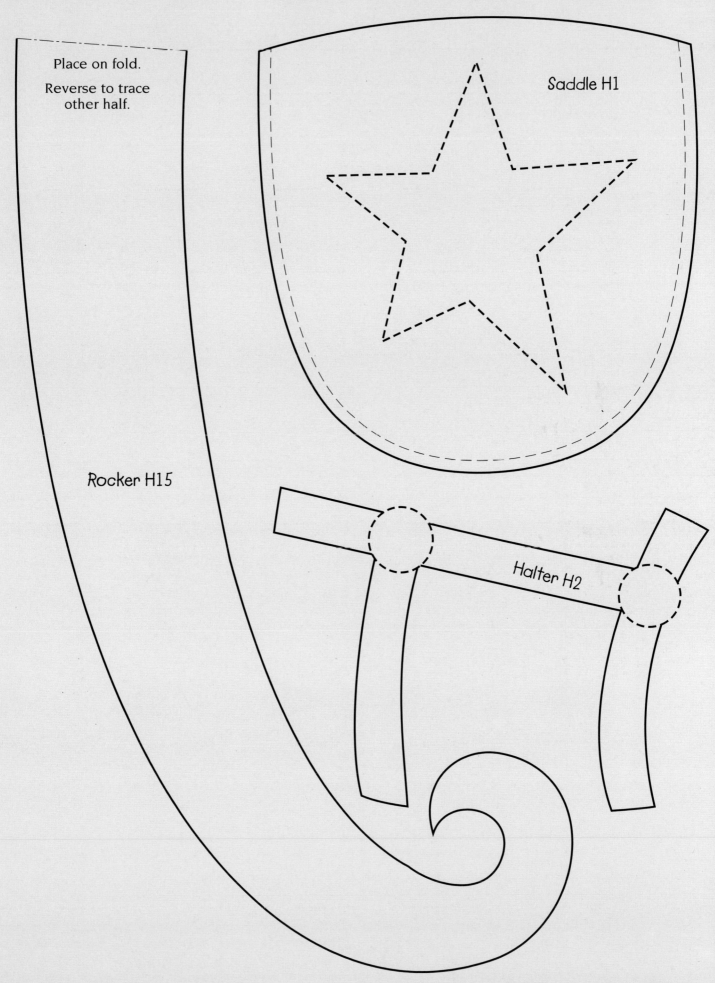

Place on fold.
Reverse to trace other half.

Rocker H15

Saddle H1

Halter H2

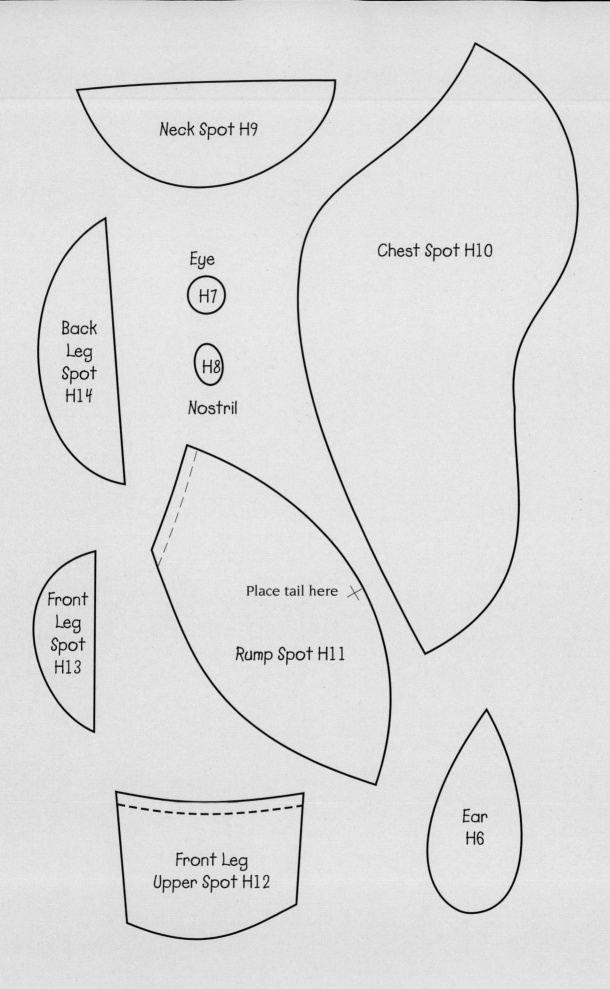

Neck Spot H9

Chest Spot H10

Eye

H7

H8

Nostril

Back
Leg
Spot
H14

Front
Leg
Spot
H13

Place tail here

Rump Spot H11

Front Leg
Upper Spot H12

Ear
H6

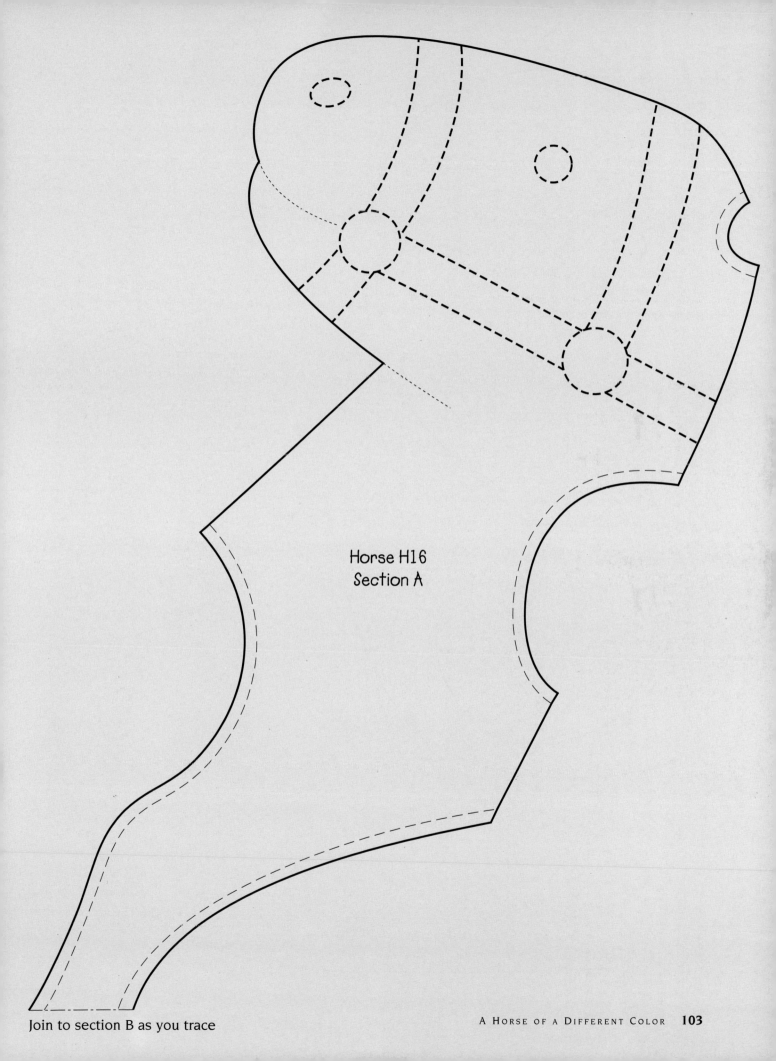

Horse H16
Section A

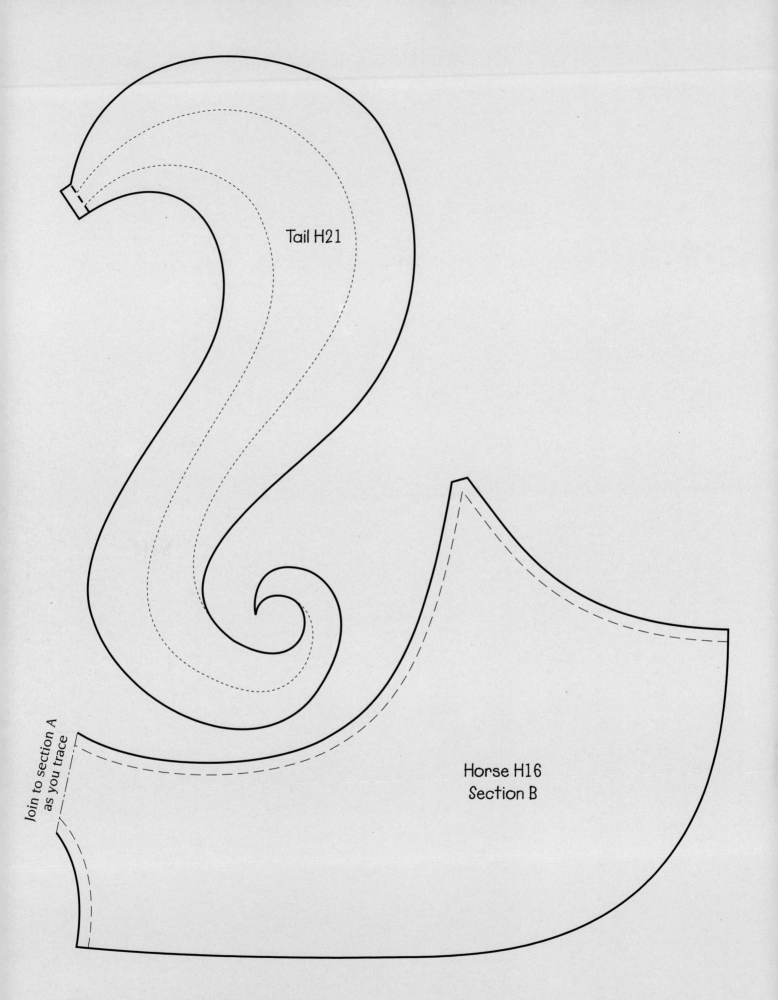

Tail H21

Join to section A
as you trace

Horse H16
Section B

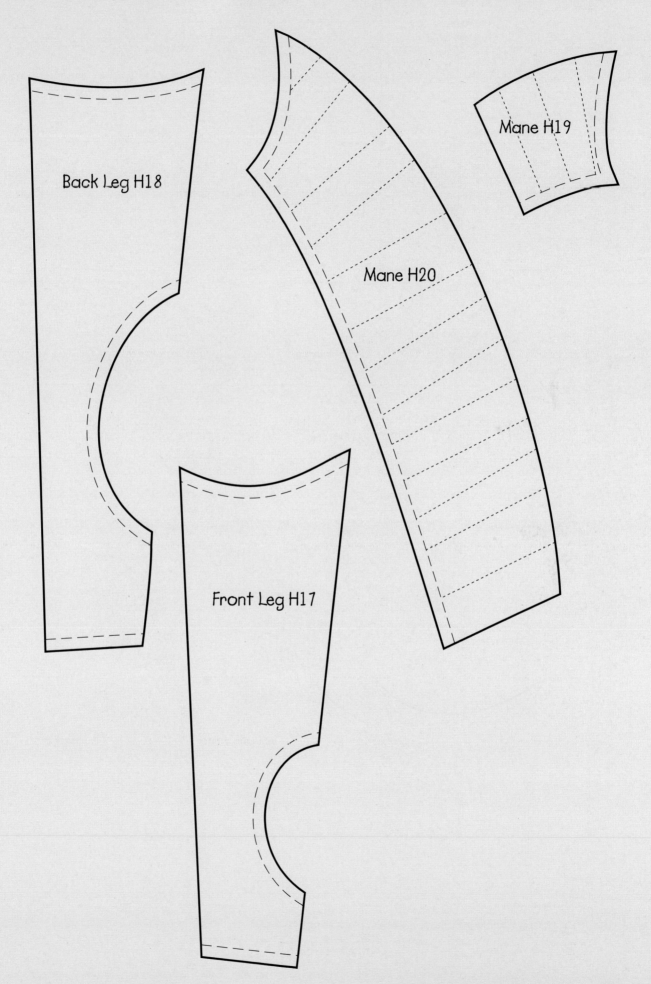

Back Leg H18

Mane H19

Mane H20

Front Leg H17

Project on Page 50

# Hugs and Kisses

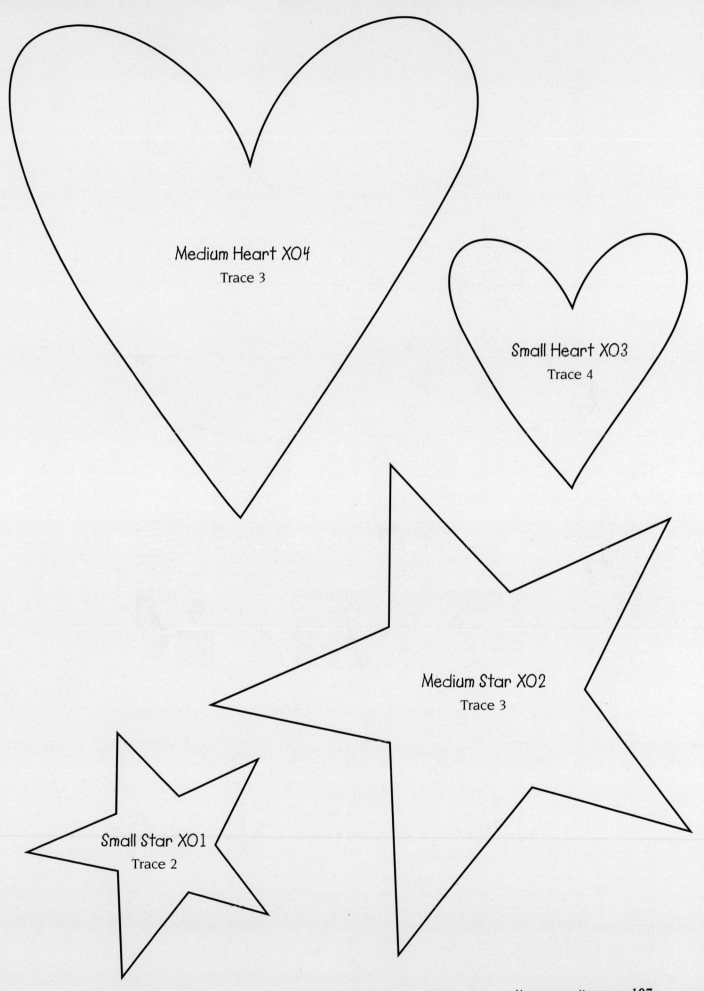

Medium Heart XO4
Trace 3

Small Heart XO3
Trace 4

Medium Star XO2
Trace 3

Small Star XO1
Trace 2

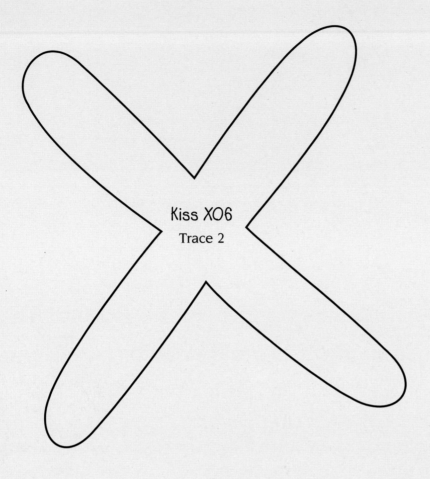

Kiss XO6

Trace 2

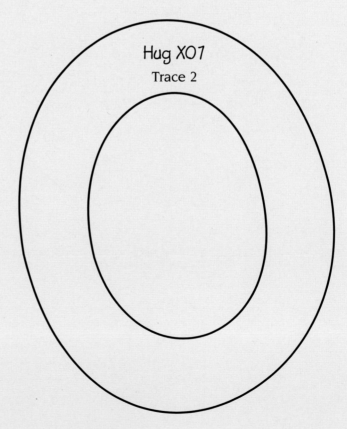

Hug XO7

Trace 2

Large Heart X05

Trace 3

Patrick Lose has spent his professional years in a variety of creative fields. He began his career as an actor and singer, which eventually led him to designing costumes for stage and screen. Costume credits include more than 50 productions and work with celebrities such as Liza Minnelli and Jane Seymour.

Photo by Perry Struse

An artist and illustrator since childhood, Patrick works in many mediums. When he sits down to "doodle" at the drawing board, he never knows what one of his designs might become. Whether it's designing fabric for his collections with Timeless Treasures or working on designs for quilts, wearable art, cross-stitch, greeting cards, Christmas ornaments, or home décor, he enjoys creating it all.

His crafts, clothing, and home decorating accessories have appeared frequently in many well-known magazines including *American Patchwork and Quilting, Better Homes and Gardens Country Crafts, Christmas Ideas, Halloween Tricks and Treats, Folk Art Christmas, Santa Claus, Decorative Woodcrafts* and *Craft and Wear.* Publications featuring his designs have reached over 18 million subscribers. Patrick currently lives in the quiet town of Van Meter, Iowa, just outside Des Moines.

# About the Author

# Resources

For quilting supplies:
Cotton Patch Mail Order
3405 Hall Lane, Dept. CTB
Lafayette, CA 94549
e-mail: quiltusa@yahoo.com
web: www.quiltusa.com
(800) 835-4418
(925) 283-7883

If you cannot find Marble Mania fabrics at your favorite quilt shop, write to:

Out On A Whim
P.O. Box 400
Van Meter, IA 50261
e-mail: PLose@aol.com
web:http://www.patricklose.com

For information on From Marti Michell Perfect Patchwork Templates, please contact:
Michell Marketing, Inc.
3525 Broad St.
Chamblee, GA 30341
(770) 458-6500

For June Tailor Gridmarker™, Shapecut™ contact:

June Tailor
2861 Hwy 175
Richfield, WI 53076
web: junetailor.com
(800) 844-5400
(262) 655-5288

# Index

# C&T Booklist

Anatomy of a Doll: The Fabric Sculptor's Handbook, Susanna Oroyan

Appliqué 12 Easy Ways! : Charming Quilts, Giftable Projects & Timeless Techniques, Elly Sienkiewicz

Art & Inspirations: Ruth B. McDowell, Ruth B. McDowell

The Art of Silk Ribbon Embroidery, Judith Baker Montano

The Art of Classic Quiltmaking, Harriet Hargrave and Sharyn Craig

At Home with Patrick Lose: Colorful Quilted Projects, Patrick Lose

Color From the Heart: Seven Great Ways to Make Quilts with Colors You Love, Gai Perry

Crazy with Cotton, Diana Leone

Curves in Motion: Quilt Designs & Techniques, Judy B. Dales

Deidre Scherer: Work in Fabric & Thread, Deidre Scherer

Designing the Doll: From Concept to Construction, Susanna Oroyan

Easy Pieces: Creative Color Play with Two Simple Blocks, Margaret Miller

Elegant Stitches: An Illustrated Stitch Guide & Source Book of Inspiration, Judith Baker Montano

Fabric Shopping with Alex Anderson, Seven Projects to Help You: Make, Successful Choices, Build Your Confidence, Add to Your Fabric Stash, Alex Anderson

Faces & Places: Images in Appliqué, Charlotte Warr Andersen

Fantastic Fabric Folding: Innovative Quilting Projects, Rebecca Wat

Fantastic Figures: Ideas & Techniques Using the New Clays, Susanna Oroyan

Focus on Features: Life-like Portrayals in Appliqué, Charlotte Warr Andersen

Freddy's House: Brilliant Color in Quilts, Freddy Moran

Free Stuff for Collectors on the Internet, Judy Heim and Gloria Hansen

Free Stuff for Crafty Kids on the Internet, Judy Heim and Gloria Hansen

Free Stuff for Gardeners on the Internet, Judy Heim and Gloria Hansen

Free Stuff for Quilters on the Internet, 2nd Ed. Judy Heim and Gloria Hansen

Free Stuff for Sewing Fanatics on the Internet, Judy Heim and Gloria Hansen

Free Stuff for Stitchers on the Internet, Judy Heim and Gloria Hansen

From Fiber to Fabric: The Essential Guide to Quiltmaking Textiles, Harriet Hargrave

Hand Quilting with Alex Anderson: Six Projects for Hand Quilters, Alex Anderson

Heirloom Machine Quilting, Third Edition, Harriet Hargrave

Imagery on Fabric, Second Edition, Jean Ray Laury

Impressionist Palette, Gai Perry

Impressionist Quilts, Gai Perry

Jacobean Rhapsodies: Composing with 28 Appliqué Designs, Patricia B. Campbell and Mimi Ayars

Kaleidoscopes: Wonders of Wonder, Cozy Baker

Kaleidoscopes & Quilts, Paula Nadelstern

Make Any Block Any Size, Joen Wolfrom

Mastering Machine Appliqué, Harriet Hargrave

Mastering Quilt Marking: Marking Tools & Techniques, Choosing Stencils, Matching Borders & Corners, Pepper Cory

The New England Quilt Museum Quilts: Featuring the Story of the Mill Girls. With Instructions for 5 Heirloom Quilts, Jennifer Gilbert

Patchwork Quilts Made Easy, Jean Wells (co-published with Rodale Press, Inc.)

The Photo Transfer Handbook: Snap It, Print It, Stitch It!, Jean Ray Laury

Pieced Flowers, Ruth B. McDowell

Pieced Roman Shades: Turn Your Favorite Quilt Patterns into Window Hangings, Terrell Sundermann

Piecing: Expanding the Basics, Ruth B. McDowell

Quilt It for Kids; 11 Projects, Sports, Fantasy & Animal Themes, Quilts for Children of All Ages, Pam Bono

Quilts for Fabric Lovers, Alex Anderson

Quilts from Europe, Projects and Inspiration, Gül Laporte

Quilts from the Civil War: Nine Projects, Historical Notes, Diary Entries, Barbara Brackman

Quilts, Quilts, and More Quilts! Diana McClun and Laura Nownes

Rotary Cutting with Alex Anderson: Tips, Techniques, and Projects, Alex Anderson

Rx for Quilters: Stitcher-Friendly Advice for Every Body, Susan Delaney Mech, M.D.

Say It with Quilts, Diana McClun and Laura Nownes

Shadow Quilts: Easy to Design Multiple Image Quilts, Patricia Magaret and Donna Slusser

Simply Stars: Quilts that Sparkle, Alex Anderson

Skydyes: A Visual Guide to Fabric Painting, Mickey Lawler

Start Quilting with Alex Anderson: Six Projects for First-Time Quilters, Alex Anderson

Through the Garden Gate: Quilters and Their Gardens, Jean and Valori Wells

Travels with Peaky and Spike: Doreen Speckmann's Quilting Adventures, Doreen Speckmann

Wild Birds: Designs for Appliqué & Quilting, Carol Armstrong

Wildflowers: Designs for Appliqué & Quilting, Carol Armstrong

Women of Taste: A Collaboration Celebrating Quilt Artists and Chefs, Girls, Inc.

For more information write for a free catalog:
C&T Publishing, Inc.
P.O. Box 1456
Lafayette, CA 94549
(800) 284-1114
http://www.ctpub.com
e-mail: ctinfo@ctpub.com